Heavenly

PERSPECTIVE

Soaking in God's Presence

STEPHANIE MONTHEY

Heavenly Perspective
by Stephanie Monthey
Copyright © 2017

DEDICATION

THIS BOOK HAS A twofold dedication: first to my precious Holy Spirit, who has been my friend, encourager, counselor, wisdom and strength. You are my teacher and my finest treasure!

Thank You for not allowing me to lean on man, instead ordaining my life to learn to lean on You. Thank You, Holy Spirit, for making me strong when I felt so weak and incapable of writing this book!

Also to my amazing husband Scott, whom I love with all of my heart! You have been a great source of loving encouragement and strength. You have inspired me in my anointing and have been my covering and protection. You spoke words of affirmation and encouragement that helped me continue to move forward in the writing of this book.

Thank you, Scott, for all of your support and the love that you have shown to me!

ACKNOWLEDGMENTS

F IRST, I WANT TO thank my husband and my four beautiful children for their patience through the years when I was preaching my sermons and sermonettes to all of you. Thank you for the fond memories we have from family soak times with Jesus! May you be forever changed and ruined by His love for you! My heart will be forever changed because of the gift that each one of you has been to me and has brought to our family and home simply by being you. My prayer is that you all will walk in intimacy with your heavenly King. I love you!

Thank you to Dennis Kresser, Pastor Heidi Kresser, and Saturate Ministries for giving me a place to freely flow in the Spirit and to use my gifts and anointing. Most of all, thank you for giving me room to fail and grow, becoming stronger and wiser each time. Thank you, Saturate Ministries team, for the prayers and encouragement through the years. All of you have been valuable instruments God has used to bring me to this place of writing this book.

Thank you, Pastors Steve and Melanie Warriner and my Abundant Life family, for paving the way in the Spirit in our region. You gave me a place to call home and fully embraced my gifts! Your love and support has made a lasting impression on my heart. Your impartation of faith and the anointing to move out in the marketplace has wrecked me and made me bold! Through this, I see your fingerprints on my life even through writing this book.

Thank you, Pastor Mitch Ivey, for the encouragement prophetically and through your sermons to dream and to set goals spiritually. You helped my dreamer come back to life! I am sure I would not have accomplished everything that I have these past five years without your timely messages. I was inspired to write this book through your repeated prophetic declarations of "There are people who are called to write books in our congregation."

Thank you, Dr. Ricky Paris, for being a father in the Spirit to me and our ministry. You understood us when others didn't.

Thank you, Linda Stubblefield, for your editing help and encouragement during the writing of my first book.

ABOUT THE AUTHOR

S TEPHANIE HAS HELPED COFOUND Saturate Ministries and also helped establish the Prophets Chamber, a ministry within Saturate Ministries. She has traveled with this ministry to conferences, churches and small groups, expressing the love of the Father through encounters with Him.

Stephanie is a speaker anointed in the prophetic; she shares a powerful gift with words of wisdom, knowledge and revelation. As she shares truth, her words carry the heart of the Father delivering faith, love and inspiration along with encouragement to the body of Christ.

Stephanie's passion is to rekindle and stoke the fire of passion for Jesus once again through encounters and experiences with Him—by soaking in His goodness, which will bring transformation and revive the weary heart in an overly busy world. Jesus' passion for us is shared through her messages, writings and prophetic encouragement.

With this call from God, she desires to establish and equip leaders, churches, small groups and businesses with the vision to bring change and transformation to their sphere of influence. Through soak sessions with our Heavenly Creator, heaven invades our hearts through God's rich anointing and His deep presence, and, in return, preparing us to be vessels to bring heaven to earth in our sphere of life.

Stephanie is married to her husband Scott, and they are the parents of four children: Shelby, Grace, Riley and Chelsey.

CONTENTS

PREFACE

by Rick Paris, PhD
President, Ministries of Vision International

I F A FRIEND INVITES you to his or her home and you graciously accept the invitation, you would expect your host to entertain, honor, and spend time with you. If the person does, then you will more than likely visit again. If, however, your friend ignores you and makes you feel unwelcome, then you will probably not be inclined to visit this person again.

The greatest need of the church in America is not more resources, more programs, or more workers in the ministry. The greatest need is more of the glory of God's presence. The problem is that most churches do not know how to host the presence of God. For that reason, there is a shallow level of His presence in the church in America.

In her book, Heavenly Perspective, Stephanie Monthey has done an excellent job of extending a most loving and gentle challenge to both pastors and church members to learn how to welcome and entertain the presence of God. She shares practical insights as to how leaders can teach their people (whether an entire church or a small group) to learn how to soak in the presence of God and hear His voice. You will be blessed as Stephanie shares what she has learned in her pursuit of the Lord's glorious presence. In addition, she has included prophetic words that she has received while worshipping and waiting on the Lord. These words reveal the heart of Jesus to His bride—a heart of uncommon and extravagant love.

Read Heavenly Perspective and embark upon the adventure of pursuing and living in God's presence—on earth as in heaven. Your life will be changed!

FOREWORD

BEING CALLED INTO GOD'S presence over eighteen years ago has brought true contentment and satisfaction to my restless heart. Enjoying Him and ministering with Saturate Ministries has given me a sense of fulfillment and joy within. Living life as a wife and a mother of four young adults has made life never a dull moment in our home and has given me pleasure and purpose. My job outside of the home of being a personal trainer, fitness instructor and nutrition coach has kept me busy, even as I also knew I was following the destiny that God has given to me.

With all that I was already doing, I had this gnawing reality that I was supposed to be doing something else. I was unable to shake the certainty. The Holy Spirit began to share with me God's desire for me to write a book. Ugh! I had a million reasons why I was not a good candidate, including lack of time and experience. With the Holy Spirit's hand heavy on my back and His foot pushing me forward as I was fighting Him, HE won, and I surrendered to the call.

Practicing what I preach in this book was essential to accomplish the book. Time management became a powerful tool with juggling all that my life entailed. Needless to say, writing a book was not on my radar, and it was really never a cherished dream or a desire because I truly did not consider myself a writer. But I see myself as John the beloved was described in the Bible in John 21:20 when he referred to himself as "the disciple whom Jesus loved," and the one who had laid his head upon Jesus' breast. I am a lover of Jesus and His presence, and I have found resting my head upon His heart and listening to Him has brought truth and revelation to my heart. I am simply a messenger to share the truth that He is given to me so that others may enjoy and find Him also.

This book is not penned from a standpoint of theology or scholarly knowledge; needless to say, a theological debate is not the issue or object for this book. I can offer no theological debate. What I can offer is what God says in 1 Corinthians 1:26 through 28:

> *"For you see your calling, brethren, that not many wise according to the flesh, not many mighty, not many noble, are called. But God has chosen the foolish things of the world to put to shame the wise, and God has chosen the weak things of the world to put to shame the things which are mighty; and the base things which are despised God has chosen, and the things which are not, to bring to nothing the things that are, that no flesh should glory in His presence.*

No, I do not possess scholarly credentials; I am merely a lover of Him and His presence. This heart-to-heart book carries the heart of the Father to the human heart. Much that has been given to me has been taught through encounters and the Holy Spirit's revelatory gift, prophecy, wisdom, knowledge and discernment. As with any prophetic word or revelation, your job is to wait before the Lord and ask Him if there is any application for your life.

My prayer for every reader would be this: that you will be able to connect with the Holy Spirit, Jesus, and your heavenly Father through a heart-to-heart communication and that you could experience the loving embraces that follow this connect. Sit back and enjoy the journey for I believe God has the ride of your life ordained for you!

INTRODUCTION

WITH EVERYTHING HAPPENING IN the world today, one of our greatest battles can be to maintain our heavenly perspective, i.e., balancing the darkness concerning world views with God's heavenly perspective and opinions. Renewing our minds through God's Word and His presence helps us to keep His viewpoint at the forefront of our lives. Spending time with Him and soaking in Him is like taking a spiritual bath and being cleansed daily. Without daily encounters with Him and His Word, we can lose our focus, become fragmented, overly busy and confused. But soaking in Him can bring His love, strength, peace and clarity to you, your family, church and business. His presence can usher in a movement that many are longing to see and experience. Transformation is the by-product of time spent with God in His presence.

You may wonder how I am so confident in God's presence. I have experienced Him, and He has brought transformation to me and my household! My experiencing Him all began when I was around 22 years of age. I was married and owned a small business in my hometown; outwardly, my world appeared fine. But deep in my heart, I hungered for more of God. My pursuit of Him began with searching and reading books. At that time, the Internet and Google were not popular research tools. In my search, God's Word came alive to me, and I spent much time reading it and worshipping the Lord.

I especially remember one special day that started as a typical one. When I came home for lunch, instead of eating I went straight to the room that became my worship room. I put in my favorite cassette, and yes, I know cassettes are from the Stone Age! I did not care to eat, which was unusual for me. I simply wanted to love on Jesus. You see, I was being so drawn to Him.

No one had ever taught me about worshipping, but worship was just flowing from my heart. During that time when I was worshipping my Lord, I began to hear someone singing with me! I quickly turned off the music to decide who was singing with me, but each time I stopped singing and turned off the music, the singing stopped. After a few times of stopping and starting the cassette tape, I became aware that the voices singing with me were angelic voices! Possibly they were singing with me to drown out the terrible cacophony I was making! Their voices made our music—even Christian worship—sound so earthly.

I can testify that no music on earth compares to the beautiful heavenly sounds and notes that I heard that day. You see, what I experienced was an encounter that God gave me that day. That special and unique time of worship touched my heart. My encounter left me speechless and longing to experience a bit of heaven again.

Fast forward a few years. I had now gained more knowledge of God and His ways and principles. But somewhere along the way, I began to travel the path of religion; I had lost my worshipful heart and childlike faith. I had more head knowledge and was trying so hard to dot every "i" and cross every "T" in my little Christian world. But something was not right in my life; walking with God was hard and no longer enjoyable! I no longer longed to worship Him. Though I did tried to read His Word, everything had become heavy and a lot of work!

I am certain that we can all attest that walking with Jesus can be difficult and that we can have tough times, but I know mine was legalistic and all self-inflicted! You see, I did not have a close friendship with Father God. In my eyes, He was stern and ready to severely rebuke me when I stumbled. Obviously, my perspective was wrong, and my view of Him was terribly skewed.

But God's loving encounter touched me all over again. I was not seeking an encounter with Him that one fall day when I was at home. Suddenly by His Spirit, He drew very near. The only way I can describe that encounter is by sharing about a little game I would play with my children. I would chase them, saying, "The kissy monster is going to get you!" I would then run and scoop them up in my arms and kiss them over and over again until they would giggle uncontrollably. Okay, I confess. We had a goofy ritual, but we had so much fun!

This little game is the very impression I received from my Heavenly Father that special day in the midst of conforming to my rules, regulations and misery. He visited me with His continual and repeated kisses. But instead of laughing uncontrollably like my children, I cried uncontrollably like a baby. I remember falling to my knees and experiencing His love In such a deep way that left me longing for more.

You see, I did not earn His approval or affection that day; I was not even seeking it. But He was watching me in my misery and decided to bring a shift to my view toward Him. Not long after that experience, our church had invited a guest speaker. As she prayed, worshipped and spoke about the Lord, I longed to have what she had. She knew God in a special way, and she spoke of intimacy with Jesus. Hearing her describe her relationship with God made me desire to know Him more deeply and to experience this same type of relationship with Him.

My longing continued as I left the meeting that night, and I prayed, "God I want to have intimacy with You like the speaker has, but I don't know how. Would You teach me?"

My pleading took me on a journey, and God, by His Holy Spirit, taught me much. But most of all, He answered my prayer and began to teach me about intimacy and the power of soaking in Him. How I longed for help on how to grow in intimacy but was unable to find the help I needed.

My prayer is that this book would be a tool to help you and everyone with whom you have influence to find God in a deeper way. May I encourage you to encounter Him through His rich presence by soaking in His goodness!

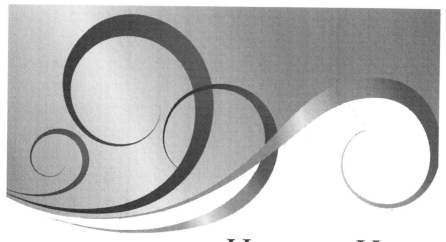

How to Use
This Book

THIS BOOK CAN BE used for reading and soaking purposes to help you experience God by "practicing" what you are learning. Mere head knowledge will not help you encounter God. I have included "Questions to Consider" near the end of most chapters. These questions and thoughts were written with the mindset to help you move out of your comfort zone and experience God with a heart-to-heart connect. This book could be used individually or as a group study format to help people who are new to the concepts of soaking and heart-to heart connect with their heavenly Father. But also keep in mind that this book will also apply to the hungry hearts who are ready to go deeper with God.

These are only suggestions as you may have a different plan for your soak time. I am including a possible format, but feel free to let the Holy Spirit lead you on how your group might look.

A chapter could be assigned weekly for the group members to individually read prior to your meeting time. Honestly, I have found with experience that this sounds easy, but busyness is an issue. Many simply do not get that assignment accomplished; therefore, they are lost during any discussion. Paraphrasing the important issues from each chapter should be shared by the leader/teacher. I would suggest considering reading the book out loud as a group. Doing so would be most beneficial so everyone receives the clear message. Each chapter highlights new concepts, but they also build upon each other. Supply your group with pens and notebook if they enjoy recording what God is speaking to them.

Once the reading time is complete, allow approximately twenty minutes or so for some soaking time where the people simply enjoy God's goodness and presence. At the end of this allotted time, stay in the soaking mode and mention that you want the people to stay in the "zone" with God. Mention the questions at the end of the chapter. Some people may want to write their answers to the questions at the end of the chapter; others may process better mentally. You may want your group to read through them on their own. Allow the people time to process and hear from God on each question. This time is for encounter and experience—not more knowledge. Perhaps you may prefer to read the questions to the group, allowing them time between each question to wait in God's presence for the answers. By all means, give them time to hear from God. Remember an encounter with God is the goal—not man talking excessively.

When you have completed the "Questions to Consider," you may finish with a prayer and comments or testimonies of what God has said or showed the people you are leading. Some may not feel comfortable to share; of course, this choice is acceptable because that is why this time is called intimacy with God.

Keep in mind, the greatest focus is enjoying God, and He enjoying you! If you choose to soak only, that will be sufficient. God will move on hearts without the questions.

As the group begins to encounter God and they feel comfortable with soaking and encounter/hearing from God, you will be prepared to set up your soak/prayer times. These times have been outlined in the latter chapters titled "Family Soak," "City and Regional Transformation," and "Stop the Train." These sessions are designed with the focus on encountering God by enjoying Him in His presence. With this purpose in mind, these encounters bring change to our hearts and to our spiritual climate by changing the atmosphere through soaking/prayer.

GOD'S EXTRAVAGANT LOVE

HAVE YOU EVER SINCERELY admired someone in your life? If so, I have no doubt when you are in this person's presence that you watch his every move, enjoy his personality, sense of humor and the way he interacts with other people. You observe this individual's movements, expressions, disposition, actions and reactions. You long to be with him because you find him fascinating. Why? Because you admire, esteem and think he is amazing and special—one worthy of emulation.

I believe that too often we often fail to realize that we have a heavenly Father who views us in this very way. He looks at us with joy, pleasure and admiration. He anticipates what we are going to do and say and how we are going to live life. He even watches the blunders that we make and knows that He's big enough to fix them. Our heavenly Father doesn't worry about our failures like we do because He's our secret admirer and biggest fan—always for us and enjoying us as His beautiful creation.

HEAVENLY PERSPECTIVE

As a husband loves, defends and protects his wife with deep compassion and passion, our heavenly Father loves with an even deeper, stronger love. A husband is devoted to his wife because of his deep love and commitment to her. Our heavenly Father, who has more of that same devotion, will defend and fight for us with passion and valor because He is committed to us. After all, we are His children. God is not a liar; He does what His Word promises. Not being a respecter of persons means that what He does for one, He will do for all—with absolutely no strings attached. No sin of humanity will ever keep Him from loving us.

This kind of love seems too good to be true. Because God is supernatural, He does not possess a fickle human love. On the contrary, His divine, heavenly love supersedes our minds and our finite comprehension. We ponder how the God who created such a beautiful world and everything in it would care and love us. But He does and He wrote the Bible, His Love Letter, to us to reveal the extent of His love to us. He didn't stop with a written Love Letter; He also sent His Holy Spirit to be our Comforter, Guide, and closest Friend. He gave us these gifts so we would find Him in a personal way to develop and enjoy a deep, abiding friendship with Him. He longs for our encountering Him and understanding His nature experientially—not simply through His written Word.

Heavenly perspective was released in the throne room by my Heavenly Father through my encounters with Him. Peering into His face has become my great reward and my finest treasure. My seeking and longing to know Him has changed my perspective, passions and dreams. My heart will be forever changed and passionately in love with Him.

His passion for us is extravagant and intense! Everyone who desires can experience Him in deep encounters with His Holy Spirit.

Through such encounters, my prayer is that many would receive God's heavenly perspective and see through Daddy God's lenses. Oh, that His heartbeat and desires would become ours. Let God take you on a never-ending journey—a passionate and thrilling ride that is un-ending until you go home to be with Him where you will eternally encounter His tangible presence and love. Most of all, may you learn His heartbeat, cares and concerns so that you may begin to receive His heavenly perspective in this broken and hurting world. In return, you can comfort and love Father God. Understanding a portion of His heart brings about a transformation and positive changes in you and your sphere of influence as He shapes and molds your heart and the hearts of those around you, leaving a legacy for the generations that will follow ours.

A TIME FAST

God's Call to a Revolution

W HEN GOD SPOKE THE word *revolution* to my heart, this powerful word became the catalyst for this book. My desire is for all of the body of Christ and for those who are yet to know Him to embrace His truth.

> *My heart longs to see a revolution—a revolution of the way man uses his time. I long to see change in how My people are consuming their lives and spending their time. My people need a revolution on what is truly considered to be important and valued. I long to reveal My goodness and to let the world taste and see that I am good—really good. Oh, not with temporal goodness, like the world's offerings, but with true goodness that lasts and does not fade away. My goodness lasts and triumphs through any opposition, and these encounters with Me leave a long-lasting impression because I am true and right and good.*
>
> *Many have a yearning for more of My depth within their spirit,*

but they have turned to counterfeits to replace these encounters with Me. The world's paradigm needs to be changed and shifted. The chasing after this world's things along with indulging in temporal pleasures prove empty and vain compared to My incredible encounters. Test Me and see the windows of heaven along with the windows of My heart and imagination.

Many glorify their idols in the music and movie industry, loving and magnifying the created ones more than the Creator, but I have a greater imagination. I long to show My creativity to the ones who could revolutionize the arts, dance, music and writing. A revolution starts with My people spending time with Me, encountering Me and finding satisfaction with My love.

Instead, programs have taken the place of true seeking, an extravagant hunger and a continual pursuit of Me. Busy schedules seemingly fill the void of the longing soul, leaving no place to seek and find Me. Running to and fro has become a bad habit and an addiction rather than a necessity. Slowing down and stopping the madness seems impossible, but it is not.

I have given every human being complete control of his choices and future plans. Stopping the fast-moving train of time must be a priority and a purposefully made choice so that I may encounter your life with love. When you slow down and come to a grinding halt, you give Me room to speak. Constant motion leaves Me with little room to move in your life. You must purpose Me in your heart as most important and set your gaze and your thoughts back upon Me. Making time for Me is all that I require. Even as you slow down, you will continue to see many distractions—even good interruptions—that will try to steal your heart and affection from pursuing Me.

My Word clearly states to love the Lord your God—Me—with

all of your heart and soul and mind. Along with that mandate, you are to love your fellow brothers and neighbors the way you love and care for yourself. I know the weakness of humanity. Distractions will always try to steal you from Me. You must remember that your first love is your first call; everything else dims in comparison. Think about this! Examine your life! Making this a priority will eliminate much stress. You have a very important call, and that call is to lavish the love in your heart on Me. Remember that as you seek Me first, all other things will be added.

My call to My people is to start spending time with Me in My presence and encountering Me. I desire for My people to wait on Me and not move until I say "Move." Will you receive the call and seek Me in a new way or will you stay with the familiar and miss My greatest movement for your life, your business, your family and your church? Seek Me, and I will give you My love and captivate your heart all over again!

I have sensed from Daddy God an imperative call for a revolution and a revival of our time that will transform you, yours, and everything about you if you will only receive the call to embrace Him. Nearly every parent longs to spend time with his children without any agenda—simply enjoying them. That very same longing permeates the heart of our Daddy God! What He really wants from His children is for them to spend quality time with Him and sincerely enjoying His presence. Our heavenly Father longs for us to be still long enough to hear His heartbeat and His desires.

He hopes for quiet moments when we will encounter Him and His love. God desires to empower us and to encounter us daily so we can carry what we have received from Him to a broken and hurting world.

After all, we will naturally begin to imitate and emulate what we see and hear our Father do while in His presence. Emulating Christ is automatic, not robotic. We become more like Him as we spend time with Him.

Many of us travel on a path that is full of church and social gatherings along with events, school activities, work, and so forth. As the schedule gets tighter with fewer free hours, a flicker of hope in the back of our minds gives rise to the feeling that "If I can get through this current week, the next week will hopefully be a little better." However, one week leads into another week, and a "little better" never seems to come. The schedule remains packed full of some really good events and activities. And with each passing day, the time you once had seems even more limited in the same 24-hours-a-day allotment.

Have we forgotten that we have control over our own schedule? When did we forget that schedules are not a written-in-stone, bound contract? Our busyness is a choice that we have willingly embraced! We all have been given the power of choice, and with each passing day, that power still remains the same. Choices need to be considered and pondered and not taken lightly because they become the driving force of our daily life. Choices set the course of our destiny; establish our business, home, church and family; but most importantly, they navigate our life. In fact, they not only set the course of our lives, but they may also affect many others around us.

If you are a leader, for instance, all who work with you generally choose to follow your pace. Every leader needs to understand that how he chooses to live his life—with jam-packed days or a comfortable schedule generally causes his followers to live life in the same way. Leaders could unknowingly be bringing peace or turmoil in their businesses, churches, homes and families by the way they set their schedules and live their lives.

Whether or not we like it, if we are too busy and stressed out, we are teaching everyone around us to accept the same; we set an example by the life we live. Whether those we have been entrusted to lead are employees, coworkers, families, church members or friends, we are sending them very clear messages. Many would agree their lives are already jam-packed; they feel stressed and the need to slow down, but they are seldom able to decelerate. This constant urgency may be a clear warning that a schedule change needs to be considered. A time fast away from the busyness may be the ticket to peace and clarity.

What Exactly Is a Time Fast?

Perhaps you are asking yourself, "What in the world is a time fast?" When most people hear the word "fast," they groan and think of going without food. A time fast is similar to most any fast. A time fast is exactly what the name implies. You are fasting some of your time so you can be with God to spend uninterrupted time with Him. Obviously, the difference is you are not fasting food or drinks unless you feel compelled to do so.

Often, we are so busy with activities and jam-packed schedules that our focus is divided when we try to spend time with our Father God. A time fast is planned with the focus of clearing your schedule from the busyness of life so you can have an extended season to focus on being refreshed, refocused and renewed in God's presence. The call to plan a time fast is for all individuals, families, churches and businesses. This fast is a getaway from the mundane matters of life to spend time with our Heavenly Father, enjoying Him and allowing Him to enjoy and encounter us.

We often feel we are doing fine with our busy and full schedules, all the while failing to realize we are lacking clarity, peace and joy. This deficit leaves us feeling drained and fatigued. Many of us have lived our lives in this way for so long, we have become numb to the unbecoming attributes of doubt, frustration and melancholy.

A time fast can awaken you to the reality of your need for rest, renewal and refreshing. Individuals, families or groups can plan a time fast. Simply look at the schedule and eliminate or rearrange activities as needed to make time for this fast. Some may find the extra time simply by eliminating screen time (television, Facebook and Internet surfing, or devices and electronics that absorb too much time daily) for a season. Planning a time fast does not mean you are required to give up something forever, but you may begin to find a nice balance at the end of your fast.

At the end of the time fast, you may find such joy and freedom in His presence that you continue to keep your schedules under control and free from being so jam-packed. Honestly, I believe the ultimate quest would be finding a balance to our schedule so more time could be devoted to spend quality time with our Heavenly Father in His presence. I believe this outcome is the desire of HIS heart!

Nearly all of the American people seem to be infected by a rampant, sweeping epidemic—a subtle lie that they need to live life at such a fast, frenzied pace because they will miss too much if their schedule is not full to overflowing. After all, our businesses or congregations might miss out on being "cutting edge." Not being involved means our children might possibly be somewhat limited and less well-rounded. Each individual in our family might become awkward and less effective in his or her sphere of influence. And some of us unknowingly maintain constant motion so we are not left to address certain heart issues.

What subtle lies the Enemy whispers in our ear to keep us running full-steam ahead! We therefore choose to run from this activity or that event, trying to be the best person we can possibly become. Our deepest ambition and desire is centered on being accepted and accomplished individuals. Although this goal seems to be sought with good intentions, somehow this fast pace usually does not bring the desired good. Embracing these mindsets leaves the by-products of fatigue, emptiness and lack of satisfaction to be addressed. Unsatisfied and discontent, we consult our schedules for the next busy day and more events to plan.

I have discovered that fear is not from God. Being driven by fear and not faith means we are out of balance. We must seek Him to dispel the fear and embrace faith to feel satisfaction.

Being whole, satisfied and receiving His anointing along with influence is a powerful gift that we can only receive from our heavenly Father. Spending time in the throne room with Him brings understanding to our authority in Him. Does this mean we abandon all of our activities and only seek Him? Probably not, but we are in a new season—a season of finding Him—of ceasing the constant doing in order to be with Him and to know Him. *"Be still, and know that I am God; I will be exalted among the nations, I will be exalted in the earth!"* (Psalm 46:10). Embracing this new season will require our making some readjustments to busy schedules and reprioritizing our lives.

You see, God has only good intentions in mind for His children, and when He requires us to be still, that means He has plans of blessing in store for us! A time fast must be established in our life so that we can clearly hear from our heavenly Father. This particular fast is a fast in scheduling our time, which requires us to clear our schedule of all interruptions in order to be with Daddy God. This time is designated for simply enjoying Him and encountering His encompassing love.

Time and Money

In addition to time, money seems to be another hot-button topic often addressed in the busyness of our world. Wise spending, careful investments, and saving up for the retirement years are daily topics of discussion. In addition to being hot-button topics, another definite correlation exists between time and money. Unlike money, time is not always considered an asset, which is a mistake made by many people.

Time must be considered as an asset because God gives us time in daily portions—twenty-four hours a day, in fact. Time is extremely precious—especially when used wisely. How this God-given asset is used matters to Him. One of the most valuable investments that can be made is spending time in His presence, preparing for the daily battles to be faced. As we spend time with Him, He imparts His restful peace and truth to us.

With the coming movement that God is preparing to bring to His people, this resource of time must be examined and used for His glory and for His purpose in order to see His kingdom advance. This concept is not addressing the time spent working for Him but being with Him. We are held accountable as to how we use our time just as we are accountable as to how we use our money. I believe adopting a time management strategy can be very similar to money management.

Questions to Consider

The following questions might help you examine the way you view time management.

- How are you using this blessing of time that the Lord is giving you?
- Are you wisely investing your time?
- Are you spending time on wasteful and unimportant matters?

- Do you have any extra time in your schedule to enjoy God in His secret place—being with Him and not doing for Him? Or is your schedule so jam-packed with work that you have no available time for Him?
- Can you scale back your schedule in any area to have more time with Him?
- Are your misusing your time in any areas of your life?
- What consumes a large amount of your time and energy and has little to no eternal value to your investment?
- Can you eliminate anything from your schedule to make a wiser investment in eternal matters?

If you find some of these questions convicting, a simple change of heart is all that God requires. When our finances are out-of-control, we discipline ourselves by budgeting our money. The same principles apply to time management. We must build up a savings account, so to speak, in the spirit by spending time in the presence of our heavenly Father. We do not want to merely get by in life; we need to have a reserve for the days to come. We need to be filled to overflowing with His precious Holy Spirit. This "savings" is only built from a place of pure enjoyment with your heavenly Father—not from a place of duty.

Eliminating debt becomes essential with financial planning. Time management is essential to spend time with God. If you spend more time on people and inconsequential matters, but you have not properly received spiritually from the throne room, you will eventually face a spiritual deficit in your life. Expending yourself through work or activities for even the good things of God must be prioritized. You may need to stop in order to invest in the throne room and build up your "savings account" once again to prepare your reserves for your future.

Building yourself spiritually must be an *ongoing* practice—not a *one-time* solution.

Each one of us experiences seasons of saving, and then God calls us to spend. His call for us to spend is not energized through the flesh but is birthed through His promptings while in His presence. Sometimes, knowing our season is difficult unless we get away with Him to seek His perspective. Oftentimes, we do not even realize how spiritually depleted we are until we spend an extended time alone with Him.

I believe Matthew 25:1-13, which details an account of five wise virgins and five foolish virgins, prophetically pictures the time in which we are living. The five wise virgins bought oil for their lamps, and the five foolish ones chose not to invest in the oil. This passage is a clear scriptural warning not to let your lamps run dry.

Today, we are called to buy "oil" through time spent in the presence of our King Jesus. He alone can supply our reserve for the days to come. No one can buy this oil for us; we must obtain it from Him for ourselves. Like the wise virgins in Matthew 25, we must heed the definitive warning not to let our lamps run dry. Jesus knew the tendency of self-willed man to try to live his life without His presence and His Spirit continually filling him.

At one time, the body of Christ could try to function without His Holy Spirit's having His complete way in their lives, but we are living in a new season and a new hour. The old has passed, and the new is upon us. God is looking for yielded vessels and carriers who will be filled with His mighty presence and glory. God is looking for those who will be amenable to being labeled as fools in this world so they can be right in His kingdom.

Possessing a deep, yielded heart to respond in a positive way to everything that He offers and to forgo what the world offers requires something consequential of us. His call for those who will say "Yes" to His kingdom is going forth in the earth. Will you be one of those chosen vessels who will yield your life to Him so He can empower, embrace and overtake you?

This entire chapter has been devoted to one of the most valuable investments we can make—time spent in the presence of the Lord. Are you willing to invest your time with Him so you may be a vessel He can use to change the world around you? The next step to encountering Him is soaking.

SOAKING IN
GOD'S PRESENCE

T HROUGHOUT THIS BOOK, I make many references about "soaking in God's presence." Understanding this concept and how to soak will be needed to be able to effectively use this book.

Soaking in God's presence has one specific meaning but has been given different names or terms through the course of history. Two older terms for *soaking* were referred to as "waiting" or "tarrying" on God in His presence. I have also heard less-formal words and more current lingo to describe waiting on God as "soaking" or "hanging out" with God or "marinating" in God. All of these terms describe a similar concept. Throughout this book, I have used more than one of these terms because they all have the same general meaning.

For a comparison word to describe *soaking*, I have chosen "tarry," a more formal word to help depict the concept of soaking. Webster's dictionary describes the word *tarry* with the following clear and direct meaning: "to delay or be tardy in acting or doing; to linger in expectation; to abide or stay in or at a place."[1] By taking these definitions and thinking about spending time with God in His presence, we can formulate a clearer picture of soaking. Allow me to put my concept of soaking in my terms: "a delay in acting or doing because of lingering with enjoyment and expectation while resting and abiding in God's goodness while in His presence." That description sounds pretty nice!

Soaking is best described as a place of bringing the mind into a place of rest, and allowing our thoughts to become fixed on our Father God. Soaking is keeping our hearts in a place of expectancy and faith, knowing that God is the rewarder of those who diligently seek Him. Soaking in God's presence is when we become less self-aware and self-focused, and the things of this world and our cares seem minimal in comparison to the greatness and awesomeness of the God of the universe. Soaking is when you get "in the zone," so to speak, with God. His presence can be sometimes tangible and close or you might simply know by faith that He is near. We receive from Him spiritually and not always intellectually. He touches our spirits with His love and presence.

Soaking in God's presence is where all our doing stops, we minister to Him, and He ministers to us. Typically, but not always, His presence is something that we are able to feel not only spiritually but also in a physical way. It could be a sense of peace or a peaceful rest, or a peaceful weight like He is all around you. The manifestations are not solely what we are after but are usually the blessings that come with times of soaking with God.

Some people may wonder, "How do you soak?" The process is very simple. Usually we would play worship music because it helps us focus on Him. Worship is the highway that leads us to the secret place with Him. You may start with high praises, but at some place, the worship music needs to be more relaxing and gentle so you can begin to move into a place of receiving and listening.

During the soaking process, the mind will become settled as you begin to take every thought captive unto the Lord. From there, you can begin to set yourself in a receiving mood, letting God touch your heart and mind and renewing your spirit with fresh passion and focus. We are often so accustomed to doing that it is hard to settle down and not do something. This soak time is designed by God to stop the doing and let Him minister to you. We then minister to Him.

All He requires from us is simply to come and be with Him. As you begin this soaking process, it may be hard to sit and not do. Because we are conditioned to go, do and work for Him, practice helps us become better at sitting and waiting on Him. Soaking is a practice that requires something of us—our time and patience.

God is omnipresent. Jeremiah 23:23 and 24 states, *"Am I a God near at hand,"* says the Lord, *"and not a God afar off? Can anyone hide himself in secret places, so I shall not see him?"* says the Lord;*"* Do I not fill heaven and earth?* "says the Lord. Because God is all around us by means of the Holy Spirit, He can be as real and near to us as we allow Him to be. How? By our becoming keenly aware of Him by acknowledging Him and paying close attention to Him. We soak in Him so we learn these valuable tools.

You see, the whole idea of soaking is to become so fixed and focused on Him that we become less, and He becomes more through us. When we become more aware of God, who has always wanted to be near to us, His presence typically becomes stronger and richer. After all, He has always been there and available. In the soaking process, we simply become more aware of Him. As we soak in Him, the Holy Spirit will teach, encounter and love on us!

CHAPTER FOUR

BENEFITS TO SOAKING IN GOD'S PRESENCE

THE BENEFITS AND BLESSINGS of soaking in God's presence are rich and powerful. I want to share some of these blessings of God that will come as you spend time soaking in His presence. May the Scriptures from His Word encourage your heart to seek Him.

1) **Clarity is restored, and confusion dissipates.** 1 John 4:17-19, *"Love has been perfected among us in this: that we may have boldness in the day of judgment; because as He is, so we are in this world. There is no fear in love; but perfect love casts out fear, because fear involves torment. But he who fears has not been made perfect in love. We love Him because He first loved us."*

2) **Faith is renewed, and fear is eliminated.** Psalm 34:4, 5, *"I sought the LORD, and He heard me, and delivered me from all my fears. They looked to Him and were radiant, and their faces were not ashamed."*

3) **Stress is released and exchanged for God's peace.** John 14:27, *"Peace I leave with you, My peace I give to you; not as the world gives do I give to you. Let not your heart be troubled, neither let it be afraid."*

4) **The overactive mind is transformed and becomes sound.** Romans 12:2, *"And do not be conformed to this world, but be transformed by the renewing of your mind, that you may prove what is that good and acceptable and the perfect will of God."*

5) **Spiritual growth and strength results.** Isaiah 40:31, *"But those who wait on the LORD shall renew their strength; they shall mount up with wings like eagles, they shall run and not be weary, they shall walk and not faint."*

6) **Wisdom and discernment is given.** James 1:5, 6, *"If any of you lacks wisdom, let him ask of God, who gives to all liberally and without reproach, and it will be given to him. But let him ask in faith, with no doubting, for he who doubts is like a wave of the sea driven and tossed by the wind."*

7) **Questions are answered, and strategy is revealed.** Matthew 7:7, 8, *"Ask, and it will be given to you; seek, and you will find; knock, and it will be open to you. For everyone who asks receives, and he who seeks finds, and to him who knocks it will be opened."*

8) **Deception is exposed, and God's truth is revealed.** John 16:13, *"However, when He, the Spirit of truth, has come, He will guide you into all truth; for He will not speak of His own authority, but whatever He hears He will speak; and He will tell you things to come."*

9) **Unity is released in our spirit, self-effort dies, and God is given control.** John 17:22, 23, *"And the glory which You gave me I have given them, that they may be one just as We are one: I in them, and you in Me; that they may be perfect in one, and that the world may know that You have sent Me, and have loved them as You have loved me."*

10) **God's love is restored and released to us.** Proverbs 8:17, *"I love those who love me, and those who seek me diligently will find me."*

11) **God will reveal His heart and thoughts to us.** John 14:26, *"But*

the Helper [Advocate], *the Holy Spirit, whom the Father will send in My name, He will teach you all things, and will bring to your remembrance all things that I said to you."*

12) God moves on our behalf through warfare and fighting for us. Exodus 14:14, *"The LORD will fight for you, and you shall hold your peace."*

WHY WAIT?

G OD'S WORD CLEARLY STATES, *"...not by might nor by power, but by My Spirit..."* (Zechariah 4:6). As we wait on God and enjoy His presence, encounters are the essence of time spent with Him. Change is available to us for our families, churches or businesses. Many have already learned the art of *doing* very well. Our children, coworkers, leaders in churches and businesses have been taught how to push and shove if they want to see things happen. Most definitely, the time comes to get moving. When God says, "Move!" we need to obey Him immediately! But the traditions that we have learned and passed down as well as the unnecessary routines of busyness not required of God must be considered and evaluated.

Sometimes we complicate life with strategies, plans and programs that keep us running, and in the end, they tend to distract us from our first love, King Jesus! Therefore, we must consider and evaluate our present day in light of the call that God has for each one of us. Sometimes, we continue on the same path because it's all we have seen and known. Paralyzing fear causes us to be apprehensive about deviating from the security of tradition.

But I sense the call from God for change—a needed revolution in how we live life and in our approach to life's problems. Simply going through the motions and copying what others have done in previous generations may not be what we have been called to repeat. Indeed, we should honor those before us and hold to all that they have taught us, but change must take place for God's manifested glory to be seen here on earth in the way He intended.

We often feel so comfortable with the familiar that change is viewed as being difficult and intimidating. But we must be brave and willing to pioneer a new path for God's glory—especially if we are the kind of leaders who have taught others to go, go, go. Perhaps the time has come to stop and reassess the path we are leading others to follow. True friendship and power comes through time spent in knowing our Heavenly Father. Indeed, programs do have their place, but encounters with Him reveal a substantial evidence of His marked difference in our life. That difference cannot be denied or changed.

As we lead others to the secret place and into His divine presence, He begins to do the work for which we hunger and long. He counsels, guides, directs and cleanses us. As we lead others, they will follow. However, the ongoing way of life He desires for us has to be a lifestyle with a passion and focus—not another program. Relentlessly seeking Him until we see God's people finding Him, knowing Him and encountering the Lover of our soul should be our goal.

Isaiah 40:31 says. *"But those who wait on the LORD shall renew their strength; they shall mount up with wings like eagles, they shall run and not grow weary, they shall walk and not faint."* In the Scripture, the correlation with waiting on the Lord and the comparison of the strong and mighty eagle was not a mistake. The eagle symbolizes freedom and justice. Their body and wing strength allows them to catch and carry prey that weighs nearly as much as they do. Along with their great strength, they possess very keen eyesight and the intelligence to avoid danger whenever possible. The comparison God makes in Isaiah's precious promise is beautiful for us as we wait in God's presence. We have access to His freedom and justice; He makes the wrongs right—even any injustice that has happened to us. He heals and restores our spirits and renews and strengthens us while daily empowering us. Keen discernment is given, and He even warns us of the plans and strategies of the Enemy. He loves us and longs for our victory in this life! The Scripture has depth and meaning and must be practiced—not simply memorized and quoted.

Waiting on the Lord goes against what seems common and sensible. God's Word declares in Isaiah 55:8, *"For My thoughts are not your thoughts, nor are your ways My ways…."* You see, He calls us to be still and to wait upon Him because He knows our human tendency to want to move and strive and work without Him. Disciplining ourselves to being still and waiting upon Him takes much self-control and patience. We tend to "feel" like we are producing fruit and making much progress when we are in constant motion, but God asks us to do the opposite to see true fruit and change. His Word instructs us to wait, to be still, to rest, and to have full and complete trust in Him. We need to trust and believe that He can produce far more than what our meager efforts can produce. Does waiting mean we are never do anything? No, what being still means is slowing down and even bringing the perpetual motion to a stop for only then can He begin to order our steps in a new way. When He then directs us to move, it will become easier as things begin to flow naturally by His Spirit instead of being forced.

Living this life of waiting and resting is an ongoing lifestyle, especially if we have been conditioned and programmed to be in constant motion. God requires us to wait so our flesh will be tempered and the self-effort will die. Our pride will come under submission to Him—the only One who can produce true fruit, and He alone truly receives all honor and glory.

Our limited attempts to produce fruit are weak and frail in comparison to His divine touch on everything. After all, don't we crave His divine touch on all that we have and do? Often, we want this touch and anointing so much that we work for it, trying to produce it by self-effort. However, all He requires from us is to behold Him, wait on Him and purely enjoy His goodness! As we do, He begins to lead, and we follow. The process is really quite simple. Through our waiting and enjoying Him, God begins to change us from the inside out with His encounters and His love. As He changes us, we begin to understand His heart a little more, and we begin to see through His eyes—not through our fleshly perspective. Priorities change, vision and clarity take place, and life becomes all about Him instead of being all about us!

Soaking and Waiting

Soaking and waiting is an art that, unfortunately, is not practiced or even encouraged much in the church or in our individual lives. But soaking and waiting on Him is the missing link to the rich anointing, personal growth and strength plus evangelism for the body of Christ. Unity in families, communities, and in the body of Christ will begin to take place as believers spend time once again seeking His face.

Many have a wrong perception of soaking in God's presence because they have simply never experienced God in this way. Hosea 4:6 says, *"My people are destroyed for lack of knowledge...."* This portion of

Knowing Him through experience

Scripture could be rephrased as follows: "My people perish for lack of experience." The Enemy will deceitfully lie and misdirect God's people to keep them from fulfilling God's divine will for their life. You see, those who have truly experienced the divine union and oneness with our Heavenly Father in the secret place will forever be marked and changed. They will never be able to walk away from this place of blessing.

From this divine place of union and communion, God's people will receive directives and clarity to take what they are learning in the secret place to their surroundings and be used in a mighty way for God's glory. The Enemy wants to propagate the lie that simply sitting and waiting in God's presence accomplishes nothing and is a waste of time. Some try it for a season, believe the Devil's lie and soon lose their desire very possibly because they never truly had the divine encounter. They write off basking in His presence as a waste of time that instead should be spent working for God and His kingdom.

The folly in this thinking is that many do not realize how much is being accomplished for God's kingdom. I understand because effecting this revolution is very contrary to the way most have been taught. Spending time with God and seeking His face by simply loving Him is the essence of His very heartbeat. One of the reasons why He created us was to enjoy fellowshipping and communing with Him. When He created us, He understood our deep need for Him.

Spending time with Him minimizes life's problems and issues. Though these concerns may not change instantly in the natural, our perspective becomes all about Him. Only then do we begin to see through His beautiful eyes. His largeness and power begins to establish the right heavenly perspective in our heart. In His presence, He may lead you to a powerful Scripture to confirm what He's doing in your life. He may speak a word of affirmation and love to give you hope and freedom to continue His work. He may release a significant vision or a dream that will transform the way you view your life. He might encounter you with His deep anointing along with His tangible presence, giving you a fresh perspective and grace to continue.

For some, He may be close and near like an always accessible, precious friend. The deep knowledge that He will never leave you and never forsake you becomes the anchor that gives you strength and courage. These encounters daily ordained by our Heavenly Father are not inadvertent or by chance. God has scheduled them on His itinerary expressly for you; however, these divine appointments are often missed merely because we fail to take the time to meet with Him.

Soaking is not a one-time event; rather, it is a continual regenerating work in which we were created to walk so we can know Him intimately and securely. Time spent in His presence brings emotional and physical healing, victory and freedom. He imparts His anointing to us and speaks destiny over our lives. Our mandate for our life becomes clear and focused as He shows us how to pray and daily directs us. I liken these times to having a daily business meeting with our boss to receive his instructions for the day. But most of all, God wants to love on us and establish us in His authority and strength.

When our Heavenly Father becomes the focal point, He fixes the broken and mends the impossible. As we soak in Him, He frees us from the burdens and the cares of our life to free us to enjoy life. Does soaking mean we do not have to be responsible and do our work here on earth? No, of course not! We are to fulfill our responsibilities under His umbrella of rest and peace. We are to follow and do what He tells us to do, letting go of what He tells us to release. Change begins to take place in our hearts as well as in the world around us. As we simply fix our gaze on Him, He gives us the abundant life that we have been seeking.

As I contemplated these thoughts, I felt God once again speak to me about the cry of my heart.

For a few moments, wait with Me. Many distractions tug at you, but your complete and steadfast gaze upon Me will sustain you now and in all the upcoming days. The road less traveled is this road of watching and gazing at your Lord. All of humanity fixes their gaze upon someone or something because I created them with a need for Me. However, many will choose to fix their eyes upon the flawed and the uncertainties, rebuffing My priceless treasures that come from regularly fixing their eyes upon My presence. All other focuses become valueless in comparison.

I am imparting to My bride a resolve to be fully committed and steadfast to Me with passion and pursuit for Me in this hour. She will not have any competing lovers with her full commitment to Me. I am calling to all who will embrace this commitment to My presence. As each person pursues Me, in return, I will bring this impartation and resolve to him. I am not a respecter of persons. What I do for one, I will do for all who will be vulnerable, humble and ask me for this gift free of reproach. This is my call to my people in this hour.

Will you receive My call? Psalm 112:6, 7, "Surely he will never be shaken; the righteous will be in everlasting remembrance. He will not be afraid of evil tidings; his heart is steadfast, trusting in the LORD."

Questions to Consider

- Are there plans/programs in your life that keep you running and, at the end of the day, distract you from your first love?

- Do you know what God has called you to be and do here on earth? If not, ask Him what He has for you to do.

- Has God called you to do something specific? Have you been too busy to obey Him? Have you ignored His promptings?

- Are you are doing something that really has no importance or value to it simply because it is a tradition? Has the time come to let go of this tradition?

- Are you afraid to deviate from the traditional path to pioneer something new? If so, what do you need to let go of to move forward toward what God has for you?

If you answered "Yes" to any of these questions, ask God to help you change. Following Him obediently will bring freedom to your heart.

"ARE WE THERE YET?"

THE FOLLOWING WORD WAS given to me by God as I was spending time enjoying His presence. May I share with you what He lovingly spoke to me?

According to Proverbs 14:12, the ways that seem right to a man lead to destruction in the end. Destruction is what many will find in the days to come if My people do not choose a relationship with the Holy Spirit. Tradition and religion are words that My people believe are far from them, but the condition of their heart is clinging to the old ways of thinking. My bride must be open to risk—the risk of not being popular, perfect or politically correct. She must be willing to break the idols of philosophy and idolatry. She must be willing to look wrong in the world's view to be right in My kingdom. She must risk being mocked, ridiculed and humiliated in order to be right before Me. No more seeker-friendly atmospheres have a place in her life! If people are true seekers, they will be seeking My truth and My Holy Spirit.

Do not mistake this issue. The thief comes to kill, steal and destroy—even in My house, robbing My bride of the true gifts of the Holy Spirit. The thief takes the true anointing and replaces it with routine and what works or fits best. No one seems to notice that dryness and stale bread have become the delicacies. Why would anyone settle for old bread when freshly baked bread is available daily? My design is manna from heaven and new wine from the Holy Spirit each and every day, but My people find it easier to eat the old instead of seeking for the new and the fresh.

Be patient and wait; don't move until I tell you to. Be still and know that I am God; this is how I roll. This is when I move. Promise to stay with Me, waiting and not moving until you know the basic principles of My kingdom. It's all very simple: wait on Me, and I will renew, refresh and restore for that is exactly what I do.

Proverbs 14:12 conclusively states, *"There is a way that seems right to a man, but its end is the way of death."* Through traditions passed down by common routines, we have unknowingly replaced our precious Holy Spirit with programs and religion with good intentions. We have desired to see God move in and through us, but these chosen methods have brought us to a place where we need to re-examine the path by which we lead and follow. Sometimes and mistakenly, His Holy Spirit has been restrained and boxed in. Waiting for His clear direction takes time and patience, which is something we don't always desire to do simply because we feel out of control and helpless. Being in this place of helplessness is exactly where God loves for His child to be. Sadly, instead of waiting for His timing and perfect will, we take matters into our own hands and begin to move and make things happen. Though our intentions are good, we sometimes move before God's exact timing, and as a result, we lack the rich anointing that He intended to bring. Praise God! His forgiveness and grace is always available to wash us and change us. If you happen to find yourself in this place, a simple change and repentance is really all that is needed to reset us and bring positive change.

Impatience

Have you ever been on a road trip with children? Probably the questions heard most repeatedly include the following: "Are we there yet?" "How much longer?" "This is boring!" In an effort to combat the redundancy of such questions, we parents try to teach our children to enjoy the journey and not to be so focused on the destination.

Impatience seems to identify many of us. And like children, we look at our journey with Father God and fix our eyes on the destination. For parents, bosses, and leaders, reaching an established destination is who we are and what we do. We seek to find ways to become more productive and set goals for reaching the destination and fulfilling the dream or the goal. This ongoing process of looking toward our destination and strategizing ways to fulfill these dreams is why we are leaders. We dream, and we put legs to our dreams. Because slowing down is contrary to our DNA and who we are, the process can be difficult.

Taking time from a busy schedule to marinate or soak in God is one matter; settling the body and the mind is a whole 'nother challenge. Taking a "ride" with your heavenly Father is simply a change that will bring lasting results for all of the responsibilities and tasks that God has given to you. Your leadership will become even more influenced by Him. Establishing a daily to-do list before you begin soaking with Jesus may be necessary. Ignoring that list until your soak time is done will be mandatory for you—if you truly want to enjoy Him. Leave all of the needs, responsibilities, and questions that you may have for a special prayer time or schedule a given time before or after your soak time for them. Enjoying Him and loving on Him needs to be your first and primary focus.

Having the time fast that I address in the previous chapter may be mandatory to help you bring a balance to your busy schedule. Having uninterrupted alone time with our heavenly Father is not like punching a timecard and putting in your required time. Enjoying an intimate time with God is losing yourself in His presence. The Lord will help you find His will for your particular situation and circumstances. After all, this time is all about Him—not duty.

For many leaders, having undistracted time can seem impossible. When duties and people are running your life instead of God, that conflict should be your wakeup call to change and rearrange your priorities. Boundaries, which are necessary, must be established so you can be the best leader God has designed you to be. Finding a balance and learning to say "No" will make you a stronger leader.

Worship will be your catalyst as you spend your alone time with God. As you take every thought captive and redirect your thoughts and mind on the Creator of the universe, He moves you from the outer courts to the inner courts with Him. Wrestling with the mind, thoughts and the heart through praise and worship becomes easier over time. Enjoying Him is your sole purpose during this scheduled time. Your mind is renewed, your spirit is refreshed, and your inner man becomes strong.

Our greatest serving is not to man; our greatest serving we can do is unto the King of the universe. As we serve and adore Him in the secret place day after day, something divine begins to take place. Our service to other people flows and becomes easier. Our perspective changes, our vision is renewed and our faith becomes our anchor. With the strength and anointing we receive from Him, we may then serve His people well.

This mandate to minister to our heavenly King is the call we have as leaders. We are then called to lead others to live the same lifestyle of finding Him, seeking Him and knowing Him. If your leading has been more about doing than loving King Jesus, the time has come to make changes for God's glory. If these traditions of doing much for God and not getting to know Him have been a part of what you have previously learned, the time has come to seek God for true transformation for those we lead.

Mark 6:48-50 depicts a prophetic picture of man's vain attempt to lead by self-effort and failing to be moved by the winds of the Holy Spirit.

> *Then he [Jesus] saw them straining at rowing, for the wind was against them. Now about the fourth watch of the night He came to them, walking on the sea, and would have passed them by. And when they saw Him walking on the sea, they supposed it was a ghost, and cried out; for they all saw Him and were troubled. But immediately he talked with them and said to them, "Be of good cheer! It is I; do not be afraid."*

In this passage, I see a clear picture for our leadership methods and the way we lead today. The Scriptures says the disciples were straining to row. Could this be a prophetic picture of our self-effort in trying to handle matters in our way or through our strategies and programs and fleshly efforts? The verse continues, *"...for the wind was against them."* Through our self-efforts, we sometimes unknowingly go against the winds of the Holy Spirit, making progress difficult and exhausting. Verse 48 notes that Jesus *"...would have passed them by* [with His miracle]." And His disciples almost failed to recognize Him (because of the hardness of their hearts).

Like the disciples, we are sometimes so inadvertently entangled with the busyness and the duties of life that we miss the moving of God's gentle Holy Spirit! May we all learn as leaders through this powerful illustration that we must be close to the Holy Spirit and not be so fixed on the natural. We cannot afford to be so consumed with our agenda that we miss Him.

Perhaps you find yourself—like the disciples—straining at the oars of life while trying to reach the dream and destinies that God has set in your heart to fulfill. And like His disciples, you have also been working by the arm of the flesh through strategies and planning, leaving Him totally out of the equation. You are not alone. Sometimes leaders long to see the dream fulfilled—even at the expense of others and God's perfect will. Once again, a simple change of heart and priorities is all that is needed.

God has a divine blueprint for each family, community, church, and business. It is mandatory that we seek Him for His divine blueprint in every area of our life. God is not looking for clones and copies. Rather, He longs for us to seek His face for His creative and unique plan in all of these areas of our life. We sometimes find it easier to copy others, but finding that success in someone else's life does not give us merit to do the same. What God has anointed for one man may not be the same for another. At this point, accessing His creative heart becomes the focal point of the soaking time.

Each church, family, business, and community will have its own unique blueprint and strategy for fulfill His destiny here on earth. When we close our ears to the world's clamor and even to the successful ones in our eyes to closet ourselves with King Jesus, we have greatness in store for our life. We have all learned from others, and most definitely their lessons and truths teach us, but the Holy Spirit must be the greatest Teacher and Mentor in our life.

The season of God's permissive will is quickly changing. Our Father is seeking people and leaders who are following after His heart, adhering to His sovereign will, pursuing a new path in the Spirit, and deviating from traditions to follow Him. Those He finds are not so consumed with being popular or seeker-friendly as they are with being Holy-Spirit friendly. Making this choice takes risk and faith, but the cost is too great to debate. We either stay with the safe and comfortable and do things our way or we abandon ourselves to His perfect will and allow Him to take complete control, accepting His rich, deep and limitless anointing.

God will bless our self-efforts that produce fruit, but the Promised Land is where His perfect will exists, and there He has full freedom to move fully with His reviving Spirit. Christ's body of believers is called to a higher calling than God's permissive will; we are called to seek Him for His sovereign will. Does this mean everything will be perfect? No, but knowing we are right in step with Holy Spirit brings stability and gives us confidence for all of our challenges. We are positioned for God's revival as well as for His fresh move to flow in and around us once again.

Questions to Consider

- What is God saying to you as you have read this chapter addressing our need to take time to enjoy Him?

- Do you have any time to get lost with Him or is your time spent with Him like punching a timecard?

- Are people running your life instead of God?

- Do you need a time fast to readjust your overly busy schedule?

- What can you do to effect a positive change in your life? Do you need to establish some positive boundaries? If so, ask God for wisdom about boundaries.

- How will your life feel more at rest and peace if you follow through on these questions? Isn't it worth it?

FAITH

A s I was soaking and enjoying God's presence one day, He simply spoke and gave me the following encouraging words:

A river of life flows from My throne. In the river, you can receive all that I have, including those things that seem broken, damaged and unfixable. Some may say those things are trash and need to be cast away. Many will give up at this point, believing their circumstances to be above My word and truth. But there is a hidden treasure for those who endure under fiery circumstances and hold fast to the unseen truth.

When the unseen becomes more powerful to you than what is seen with your natural eyes, you will know you are beginning to walk in My Spirit. Then you will begin to taste a glimpse of heaven. What may seem most important and what you often hold most dear are the fleeting and the temporal. Much of what is eternal is unseen to the natural eyes and can only be accessed by faith, but the eternal holds insurmountable blessings and rewards. The stakes are high when living this life of risk coupled with faith.

I created My children to find pleasure in this place. When faith and My Word meet, an amazing fulfillment to answered prayer takes place. Much like an individual might find adventure as an enjoyable high, My children can find even more of a "high" as they step into this place of new realms of faith in Me. Being taken on this adventure, which offers a lifetime of contentment and fulfillment, is better than any thrill the world has to offer.

My child, are you willing to take the challenge of risk and faith? Will you believe in Me and trust Me?

Romans 8:6-8, *"For to be carnally minded is death, but to be spiritually minded is life and peace. Because the carnal mind is enmity against God; for it is not subject to the law for God, nor indeed can be. So then, those who are in the flesh cannot please God."*

Faith is the unseen substance that becomes the essence of how we live, the reality of what we think and often the success of what we do. Without faith, we approach our heavenly Father with a timid or unworthy attitude. The Word says in Hebrews 11:6, *"But without faith it is impossible to please Him, for He who comes to God must believe that He is, and that He is a rewarder of those who diligently seek Him."* Thus, our knowing-Him-intimately approach to our heavenly Father and Jesus must be the same as it is for salvation. We accept the grace gift extended to us by complete faith. Jesus gave us the gift to enter the Holy of Holies the day He died on the cross and shed His blood for us! The result of the veil's being torn is this amazing free gift which was given to us. We can have deep fellowship and conversation with this beautiful man called Jesus. We can have communication with our heavenly Daddy who cares about every need we have, yet He created the entire universe in which we live. We cannot earn His acceptance through our actions or works in the natural, but His Word says we can please Him through our simple faith in Him.

As we continue to believe in Him and His goodness, He will reward us for diligently seeking and finding Him. Our reward is more of His character, attributes and His wisdom as His heart will be revealed to us. To know Him is our greatest reward! Every time we encounter and experience Him results in His Holy Spirit's touching our spirit in a way that changes us. He knows how to gently and uniquely encounter us with His love. By these encounters, we are changed by His goodness.

Romans 2:4 says, "...do you despise the riches of His goodness, forbearance, and longsuffering, not knowing that the goodness of God leads you to repentance?" He cleanses us through His great love toward us, through His rhema Word and through His presence. Faith becomes the key element when we come to our Lord, and we desire to know Him in a deeper way. He has a special gift daily that He wants to release to us individually or corporately. He waits for us with expectancy, and He desires the same faith and expectancy from us. He loves to feed the hungry soul. He is not looking for a forced hunger or for someone who is trying hard; rather, He is looking for a heart coming to Him with faith who knows that he will receive only good from his heavenly Father.

Zephaniah 3:17 says, "The Mighty One, will save; He will rejoice over you with gladness, He will quiet you with His love, He will rejoice over you with singing."

"Rejoice over you" literally means "dance, skip, leap and spin around in joy." God dances with shouts of joy over us! How much more should we dance with joy since He is in our midst? "Rejoice" is translated from a Hebrew word that Strong's defines as "A primitive root: **properly to spin around (under the influence of any violent emotion)**, that is, usually rejoice…:— be glad, joy, be joyful, rejoice." The Hebrew word means to "spin around under violent emotion," or basically to dance. So Zephaniah 3:17 is more accurately translated as "Yahuwah, your God in your midst, the Mighty One, will save; He will rejoice over you with gladness. He will quiet you with His Love, He will dance over you with singing." Zephaniah 3:17.[2]

As we encounter our heavenly Father and anticipate time with Him, we can find peace, knowing He longs to spend alone time with us. He is excited and looks forward to this uninterrupted time with Him.

The Word does not mention requirements such as being perfect and working hard to please Him so He will rejoice over us. Merit is completely removed. The good, the bad, and the ugly part of us is still viewed through His eyes of love in the same way, and He anticipates being with us. His heart looks at us through Jesus' finished work on the cross, and He rejoices with joy and sings/dances over us. Through God's Word, we can see that getting to know Him in a deeper way is not contingent upon our good works and achievements. His Word was established and set before we were ever formed. His Word, which was for us before we ever took a breath and sinned, has not changed.

We can approach the throne of our Lord with the same excitement and anticipation that He has for us. Expectancy is the catalyst for encounter. When we are in His presence and He teaches us, we begin to change our perspective on life and God. He removes the negative thoughts, fear and worries of life and replaces them with hope and faith, filling us with His peace and giving us the confidence that He will be happily at our side.

Marinating in His goodness helps us to have a daily vision correction. He brings His truth into sharp focus, so the world's residue is washed from us and does not distort our vision and our earthly purpose. As we expect and believe in Him through His Word, we can approach Him with full confidence, knowing He will empower us for all that we will need for the day. Exodus 14:14 says the Lord will fight for you, and you shall hold your peace. As He wars and fights, we rest in the peace that comes from God when we encounter Him daily. Then we carry His peace and calm with us as we keep our hearts fixed on Him throughout the day. This scripture reveals that God is caring for matters far beyond what we can understand or see. Ours is a place of faith, trusting He is moving and fighting on our behalf!

A beautiful experience begins to take place as we spend time with Jesus. This communing is not only *experiential*, which means "we experience Him and converse with Him, He also begins to reveal His secrets to us. As our relationship deepens, He trusts us with His heart matters. Because God's heart matters, the matters of His heart really do matter. The "thought-matters" are meaningful and have value; the important "concerns-matters" of His heart should also matter to us.

The deep things of our hearts are ever so gently exposed only to receive His perspective and thoughts about circumstances and situations that are precious to His heart as well. Most importantly, He shares His emotions, viewpoint and compassion for others.

God carefully and skillfully corrects our vision so we can see matters through His lenses of love—not through the skewed vision of sin, criticism or judgment. He brings a clear and loving perspective on all of life, and we can begin to see life from His point of view. Being lost in His goodness daily has a supernatural effect on us. He is love, joy and peace, and this exchange begins to take place in His throne room. As we drop off our "dirty laundry" so to speak, which can be negative attitudes, concerns and fears, He exchanges them with more of His character.

Through the smallest seed of faith, God can begin this ongoing, never-ending journey. Encounters begin to take place as His heart uniquely touches ours as only He can do. The Holy Spirit moves creatively and differently to continue to reveal Jesus and our Heavenly Father to us. The journey is unending, our heart is revealed openly and transparently to Him, and in exchange, His heart is likewise revealed openly and transparently to us. A back and forth, never-ending dialogue through these opened heart portals like a ping-pong game brings a more intimate understanding of Him.

When we begin to experience our Lord through encounters, His Word becomes living, real and tangible and brings needed strength and stability. These encounters coupled with God's Word are vital to every believer. Soaking and basking in intimacy with our God frees our spirits and transcends the understanding of our intellect. We cannot think our way into an encounter with God; rather, the Holy Spirit has to touch our spirit, bringing divine transformation to us.

Our Heavenly Father created us with a hunger to experience Him in a deep and powerful way. We were not created to have fellowship solely through His Word, but from His Word coupled with His encounters. We were created to meet with Him and to feel His affection and love toward us.

We were created to hear His voice and to know Him. This relationship is mandatory with those we love here on earth; they need our time, love, affirmation and affection. Any earthly relationship without these loving encounters would be void and shallow. Should we expect our relationship with our Heavenly Father to be any different? We likewise need His affection, encounters and love. His affirmation is mandatory for us to become all that we have been created to be and do, and the journey starts with the small seed of faith and our willingness to seek to know Him.

Questions to Consider

- Do you feel timid or unworthy in God's presence? Ask God to show you the lie attached to that improper mindset you are believing. Ask Him, "What lie am I believing?" Wait for Him to show you.

- Do you feel like you must work for God to gain His approval? If so, ask God to reveal to you what lie you have embraced to receive this false mindset. Wait for Him to reveal this deception to you. Try to relax and receive from Him.

- Is God asking you to do something that requires risk or is stretching you?

- Do you believe God truly delights in you and sings over you? If not, ask Him to encounter you and give you a life-changing reality of this concept. He wants to encounter right now; wait for Him.

FEARLESS

W E LIVE IN UNIQUE and challenging times here on earth. Fear seems to be a sweeping tactic of the Enemy to cripple people and prevent their being all that they have been called to be. Our call as believers is to be free of the fear and the ensuing worries which choke out the life that Christ has given to us. Finding freedom from anxiety, concern, and distress can become an ongoing battle as much around us is screaming this message of fear and worry coupled with hopelessness.

One of our greatest weapons of warfare in this season will be the joy, peace and faith that we carry. These attributes cannot be mimicked or faked for the genuineness will be seen by all—believers and non-believers alike. Our complete trust in King Jesus will bring a radiant presence that cannot be denied by the world. His guidance and comfort in times of fear is our inheritance. We are called to bring this same freedom from fear to the world. What He imparts to us in the secret place, we are to impart to this world in need of a Savior.

From finances, marriage, and job circumstances to rearing and training children, we have a plethora of arenas to process and consider. In a world filled with violence, terrorism, and uncertainties, our natural tendency is to worry and fear. Of course, the world encourages us to follow this natural tendency. Through our relationships and the media, we can sometimes feel bombarded with the negativity that surrounds us.

With this onslaught of negativism, embracing God's perspective is mandatory; otherwise, we will not be any different than the world. Chiming in with the worry, fear and negativity will only cause us to become powerless chameleons. We can try with all our human might to be positive and different; however, without a true transformation, we will continue to battle with the fear, worry and negative mindsets.

At this point, encounters and God's Word become transformational and life-changing and bring a life-giving difference. His viewpoint becomes all-consuming; His authoritative Word and perspective generates everything that we see and do. Confidence in what He tells us in the secret place and how He promises to move in our lives becomes the driving force of who we are and what we do daily. At the point where many will become fearful and stop, we can walk boldly through this life because we have confidence in what He speaks to our heart.

Through many years of our marriage, four children, and a single income, my husband and I struggled financially. From job loss to circumstances out of our control, ours seemed to be an intense battle that was beyond our capability of controlling. In the natural, we followed God's Word through tithing, saving and living within our means. But the struggle continued to rage unendingly. Through the years, the weariness of fighting this battle became stronger, and at times, the fear became all-consuming. Frequently wondering what we had done wrong, we would seek God for answers and solutions to this ongoing struggle.

One night as I was sleeping, God gave me a powerful dream. In the natural, I had always been a fairly good math student, so the dream was very puzzling to me. In my dream I was given a math test, but I was unable to find the formulas to complete the problems. As hard as I tried, I could not solve the math equations, and I found myself very frustrated in my dream. The scene in my dream then changed, and I saw a bed where I could rest and sleep. At that point, I awakened from the dream.

As I pondered the meaning of the dream, I felt God was saying that no formula in the natural could solve my problem; rather, I needed to rest in Him and simply trust Him to take care of our finances. After all, simply resting by faith and abiding with Him is the solution to all of life's tests. We must follow God's principles, but by no means are we released from the responsibility of doing our part. We have been called to walk with integrity and to do what is right in the eyes of God and man. When you have done everything you can do in the natural, your greatest warfare against the Enemy will be the rest, peace and faith that you embrace in times of struggle and trials. We receive this rest and peace from Him as we marinate and soak in His presence and His Word.

This dream became a reality months later when the weight of our financial struggle intensified. My husband had an accident that removed him from the work force for nearly three months. Fear and a multitude of questions began to escalate in my heart and plague my mind. "How will we pay for the trauma surgery on my husband's foot?" "How will we pay for all of the additional bills when we are already living from paycheck to paycheck?" "What will we do when there is no paycheck?" Wrestling and fighting with fear, I finally become weary and exhausted. I could see this picture in the spirit of my limp and weary body lying in Father God's hands. The fight was over; the only one recourse I had was REST and let God take over. As I gave up, God spoke this powerful and life-giving word to me:

You have received your financial breakthrough. When fear no longer has a hold and power over you, then true breakthrough takes place. When you trust and believe and rest in Me, that is a true spiritual breakthrough.

You see, nothing had changed in the natural—not even for several months later. But everything changed in my heart that day when I was pressed to trust Him fully because I could do nothing else. I was weary from the fear and the anxiety I was embracing—the "test" I kept failing in my dream. All He wanted from me was complete faith and trust in Him. God was so faithful to provide financially for us during that season.

Need a Spiritual Breakthrough?

Truly, you can have all the money in the world and not be financially free. If you are still seized with an overwhelming fear of losing your money, you are not walking in true freedom and financial breakthrough. The principle applies to every area of our life in this avenue of fear. True breakthrough and freedom is first given to us in the spirit when we are free from the stress, the worry and the anxiety. Unfortunately, even in the Christian arena, we are told to strive for financial freedom so we never need to worry about our future. If God allows that freedom to take place in our life, how wonderful! But if the root of struggling with fear is still in our heart, we still need to be free from the fear for true breakthrough.

Needless to say, within a few months we did receive a financial breakthrough in the natural. God is after our heart—not our comfort. I sense from the Holy Spirit that this prophetic dream is also for the body of Christ. Though your struggles may not be financial, we all have our own individual, tailor-made battles. When we have done everything we can do in the natural, our greatest strength, deliverance and freedom lies in Him and Him alone. We must set our gaze completely on Him, trusting Him fully.

As we look to Jesus for our freedom, true spiritual breakthrough in our spirit will take place. In exchange, we can trade our worry and receive freedom and victory—no matter what our circumstances tell us. True victory is the genuine freedom we experience in our spirits. Anyone who needs healing physically and has not yet seen the full manifestation of the healing but is truly walking in God's peace and rest has experienced a divine breakthrough and victory. Is resting in God's ability to heal not a powerful testimony for all to see? Our ways are not always God's ways. Yes, I will always believe in God's healing power, but if the healing doesn't come, watch for God's beautiful miracles in another form. All of life testifies of His attributes and goodness being displayed.

In a world that struggles with terrorism, violence and crime, we believers have the greatest weapon of warfare—the availability of the peace of King Jesus and being steadfast in Him. Knowing that He has our back and that all things work together for our good, we can walk in complete peace. Whatever the outcome is, His name will be exalted. He is our victory, and He is our strong tower. If He is for us, who can be against us? Through life or death, we have victory. Terrorism is simply one of the Enemy's tactics to bring fear and terror to our hearts. Unfortunately, the aftermath of terrorism has been doing a fairly good job of elevating fear throughout this world.

In these troubled times, we must remember who created this world and every human in it. As believers, we must not lose our perspective of who is really on the throne. Because we have read the end of the Book, we already know who wins! Our job is to help usher in His presence, peace, and truth here on earth. Faith in Jesus and His Word must be the unseen substance that carries us throughout our days. The radiance of His presence and the peace that we carry will be a testimony that speaks volumes.

Neither the world, man nor the government can solve our problems. We must not look to mere human leadership to bring the changes that we desire. With God's wisdom and guidance, which He has abundantly given to His people, positive change can begin. God's Word declares this change starts with His people:

> *"but you are a chosen generation, a royal priesthood, a holy nation, His own special people, that you may proclaim the praises of Him who called you out of darkness into His marvelous light; who once were not a people but are now the people of God, who had not obtained mercy but now have obtained mercy."*
>
> (1 Peter 2:9, 10)

Change starts with us—in our hearts, through our perspective and the voice that God has given to us. We each have been given a sphere of influence; we must boldly walk in this influence and favor, loving the people around us and fearlessly sharing the deep truths that He has deposited within each one of us. As we fulfill the mission He has designed for us, change will be inevitable. As a result, God's kingdom will advance and be established in a new way as He has always intended.

The word unrest seemed to be the point of issue that God desired to illuminate one day during one of my quiet times with Him. I had been struggling over a troubling situation, so He lovingly enlightened my heart once again to His truth. The following is the perception He shared with me:

My child, the unrest in your heart is your greatest battle. You love Me and trust Me, now rest in Me. My rest is not easy to understand with the human mind; it surpasses the intellectual debates and becomes a resounding faith in the unknown places of your life. The battle becomes real when your circumstances exist without any indication of change in your natural surroundings. At this point, the collision in the spirit takes place. The faith battle begins: My word and truth versus your unsettling circumstances. This is the ultimate test of rest and abiding in Me. The winner is the one who becomes great in your eyes.

The truth is, I never change; however, the focus of your gaze must change. As you keep your gaze steadfast upon Me, the rest of life naturally becomes easier. Your greatest success will be making Me larger than life in your heart and mind. As you do, My Word becomes real. Nothing will be impossible in your life when you remain fixed on Me, steadying your heart next to mine. If you were able to peer through the windows of heaven, you would see that the greatest champions in My eyes are those who walk in continual communion with Me, keeping their gaze full upon Me. The distractions of life do not overtake them because they are fully resting in My promises and truth.

My child, success in My kingdom is walking intimately close to your King. The world has many kingdoms governed by many human rulers and kings, but man was created to walk with Me. However, false idols too easily take their affections. As My child, you have My divine DNA, and you were created to walk and live in My continual rest and love. This destiny is yours in life. Your highest quest is to know Me and to abide in My everlasting love, rest and peace. With this pursuit, evangelism and reaching the lost will become a life-style—not a place of striving.

Rest in My goodness, and I will open the windows of heaven for you. Know that My love is deep and wide. Step into Me in a new way. Psalm 16:11, "You will show me the path of life; in Your presence is fullness of joy; at Your right hand are pleasures forevermore."

Questions to Consider

- Do you have any areas in your life where you struggle with fear/worry and still desire full control? How is that working for you? Are you enjoying life? How will life feel if you surrender those areas?

- What has become enlarged in your thinking and made God shrink to super-small? Is it time to set your gaze back on Him in this area of your life?

- For what divine breakthrough are you believing God? Resting in His goodness will bring peace during the process.

- Can you truly trust God and give Him full control? If so, relinquish that full control to Him and start a new day of peace and resting in Him.

CHAPTER NINE

THE POWER OF CHANGE

ENERALLY SPEAKING, NEARLY ALL of us would agree that change in a positive way needs to take place in families, individuals, churches, business and government. Many studies are continually being conducted, and people feverishly work to bring about positive changes to make our world a better place. These strategists and their formulated approaches are indeed important. We are living in a world that offers much in cutting-edge technology, telecommunications, scientific knowledge and medicine. Even with all of the efforts to effectuate positive change through these areas of advancement, this nation continues to see a sustained moral decline. Now reaping the repercussions of a lack of character, this nation is now experiencing a downward spiraling of morality, integrity, honor, and uprightness.

As I began my journey into intimacy with my Heavenly Father nearly eighteen years ago, the Lord began to share with me about this decline in society and the coming darkness. He emphasized the importance and the power of soaking in His presence. As Father God began to speak of the impending darkness, He knew of the solution to the upcoming problem before we could even see the fullness of His predicted moral decline and the increased manifestation of sin here on earth.

Our Daddy God is continually warning us to protect ourselves so we can succeed and experience a complete victory. His warning was clear then and still rings in my heart years later. His forewarning was simply instructing us to become intimate with Him and begin to spend time soaking in His presence and learning about His heart. Implementing this discipline would be the lifeline for all believers during this ensuing time of darkness. He began to share with me that because of the deception, disillusionment and twisted truth, His people would need to spend even more quality time with Him. Staying close to Him in His presence and His Word would be the perfect antidote for the encompassing darkness. Without these encounters, many will be deceived, fall away and embrace the world's truth—instead of God's truth.

His mandate was clear to me, and embracing Him is our ticket to victory during this season of our lives. I sense from the Lord that knowing Him was not about comfort and preference; rather, soaking in Him will be mandatory for survival in the coming days. Everyone who embraces this call to intimacy in His presence will walk in His divine favor and goodness during these times of darkness. But those who refuse to become intimate with Him, stay close to Him and choose the world instead, may suffer the consequences of deception and confusion.

Years ago, God began His gentle nudging in my heart to spend time alone with Him. Additionally, He began to encourage me to share with others about His presence and intimacy. By simply enjoying Him through worship, soaking and reading His Word, He began to teach me the matters of His Spirit, how He moves, what He likes and dislikes, even revealing portions of His discernment. The more I learn of Him and love Him and the closer I get to His heart, I can truly see how little I know of Him. I am stirred to find Him and to understand His ways even more.

We never arrive and learn it all; we only have a closer snapshot of our own hearts and our desperate need for Jesus to make us more like Himself. This call is not for a few; it is for all who will receive it and pay the price to find Him and to know Him. The call is very simple, but also very profound. I sense from the Holy Spirit and see with my eyes that the predicted darkness of which the Lord spoke years ago is now being evidenced here on earth. His presence and Word is our shelter, our refuge and our filling station for these tenuous times.

What was once a good idea, i.e., getting to know Him intimately, has now become a mandate and will be obligatory for survival. Without His watch care, we are left vulnerable, unprotected and prey for the Enemy. This is a season for Psalm 91:1, 2, which declares,

He who dwells in the secret place of the Most High shall abide under the shadow of the Almighty. I will say of the LORD, "He is my refuge and my fortress; My God, in Him I will trust."

This passage is a prophetic picture of the power of His protection that we will receive from our Father in these last days. Psalm 91 further proclaims that if we dwell in Him in the secret place, we will receive divine protection and deliverance from the Enemy's attacks. Verses 3 and 4 declare, *"Surely He shall deliver you from the snare of the fowler and from the perilous pestilence. He shall cover you with His feathers, and under His wings you shall take refuge; His truth shall be your shield and buckler."* Our part in receiving the benefits that God's Word is addressing in Psalm 91 is simply going to that secret place in faith, abiding there and trusting in Him without fear. This lifestyle must be continually practiced. Encountering Him is not a quick visit and on to the next scheduled event. Our Father God is not our "McJesus" like a McDonald's fast-food restaurant. No, He is a God who deserves our life and requires our attention when we spend time with Him.

We have access to His transformational change in our life as well as in the world around us. The power lies in King Jesus; we have full access to Him as we yield to His unfathomable work in our heart through His presence. Accessing the change only He can bring requires priority time on our part. In our microcosm, we often tend to make life rather complicated, and the demands of our time have reached a level of stress, which many would agree needs to be changed. If we, as a society, continue down this path of busyness and constant stress, the road could become increasingly difficult and rocky. Positive change is needed! Even with the plethora of self-help books, seminars and resources within our reach, the statistics of this nation's evident moral decline prove that, even in the churches, real transformational change is acutely needed.

We often become overwhelmed with the big picture because it is too big for us. Passivity never brings positive change. God wants us to break down life's problems into His way of thinking. Only then can we start to effect change in our own lives, families and church, our business or workplace and lastly our cities and states.

The same concept applies to looking at the end result instead of enjoying the journey. Sometimes we are overwhelmed before we begin and simply stop, assuming that our small efforts will make little to no difference in the world in which we live. In short, we have looked at the end result instead of enjoying the journey.

The power of change can start with you as you begin your journey to the secret place with Jesus. As you spend time alone with Him, your heart will begin to change. When and as you change, something amazing begins to transpire; the people around you become affected by this positive change. When you hang out with Jesus, He "rubs off on you." The lingering effects of being in His presence begin to "rub off" on those around you. Therefore, the cycle continues out of your own investment of time in His presence; your expenditure of time begins to multiply. When real change happens in your heart, the benefits have lasting effects on those who are a part of your world.

I have enjoyed seeing revival in a corporate setting, and the experience was transforming, electrifying, and left me longing for more of Jesus. With this deep hunger kindled in my heart, God set a passion and hunger in me to see Him likewise move in my church, city, state and beyond. I would cry out to Him for this and still do. But through the seeking and longing for this corporate move of God, the Holy Spirit sweetly began to move on me, teaching me a very powerful lesson.

He began to speak to me about digging my own personal wells of revival. He specifically spoke to me, reminding me that He cannot be stopped in my life. He shared with me the concept of personal revival. I realized that I could daily live in His reviving, rejuvenating and life-giving power—in spite of my surrounding conditions or the direction that the local church or the world's institutions were heading. I could live, breathe and dwell in my own personal revival all day, every day! As this concept was new to me and one I had never been taught, I began to press into Daddy God to receive the added "more" that He had for me.

Through the years I have continued to seek Him for the more that He has, and He is so faithful to fill and revive me. I now walk in personal revival with my King Jesus. The Word states in Acts 10:34, *Then Peter opened his mouth and said: "In truth I perceive that God shows no partiality."* Because God is not a respecter of persons, He does not play favorites. Everyone has the grace and blessing to walk in his own personal revival. That walk starts by faith and hunger for Him. When you ask, you will receive, which is where the power of change begins to take place. Not only is your heart changed, He gives you this desire to bring change around you. He gives us His keys to His kingdom in His inner courts. He releases anointing and imparts callings in His inner chamber. Wisdom and truth are revealed, and strategies to life's most difficult problems are unraveled and revealed in His presence.

Often we choose the hard road of life by doing things our way. Simply admitting that we need more time with our Heavenly Father and agreeing that all of this truth would bring benefits to our lives is not enough—especially if we fail to make this simple but profound truth a reality and a lifelong pursuit. Unfortunately, many do not realize that much of what we do and the very reason we have been created is for this one purpose: to know Him and to make Him known. In return, out of this place of truly knowing Him, we are called to make Him known to the world around us. He shows us how to do this in a casual, everyday life when we spend time with the greatest revivalist, King Jesus.

If Jesus is the greatest revivalist who ever walked this earth and He now lives in us, what does His presence mean for you and me? Our destiny is not only to walk in our own personal revival but to carry revival with us every day of our lives. Effecting revival is our calling, our destiny and our promising future. The power to bring change in our world rests within each one of us.

Isn't it time to see real change in your own life as well as in the world around you? What's holding you back? Why wait? The time is now!

Questions to Consider

- How important is it for you to know God in a deeper way? Are you willing to "pay the price," so to speak, in the spirit to find Him?

- Do you have internal peace and contentment? Do you believe God has a deeper, more fulfilling life for you? If so, what step can you take to move toward a closer walk with Him?

- Are you ready for change and to walk in personal revival? It starts with your asking and positioning yourself before Him. He is willing to come; you only need to stop and give Him room to move.

- Dream. If you make room for Him to move in your personal life, how will this affect change in your world? Is affecting change worth it to you? Will you commit to the "more" that God has for you?

THE REVOLUTION
BEGINS NOW

W HEN WE WHOLEHEARTEDLY EMBRACE the concept of soaking, the power and the anointing begins to increase as we begin to implement His simple truths into the lives of those around us. We have the opportunity not only to experience the Holy Spirit individually, but we also have the power to bring others into His presence and see them experience Him as we do. The anointing is rich, and the powers of darkness begin to lose their influence and power in our lives. Change is, therefore, inevitable.

Soaking, worship and beholding our Heavenly Father is the greatest form of warfare and prayer that we can experience here on earth. When everything around us is in the midst of chaos, our pure worship and adoration to our Heavenly Father stops the chaos. The warfare that the Enemy wants to throw at us no longer has momentum or strength. Being with Him is powerful and effective and is a joy for all who participate! Taking this concept of soaking to churches, families, businesses and small groups will bring change and transformation.

God is longing to bring a movement to His people which will revolutionize our thinking, traditions and habits. But most importantly, this resulting transformation will bring His body of Christ nearer to see Him, experience Him and embrace His glory.

This movement will not be about man's being lifted high or exalted. Rather, man will be humbled and simply usher in His Holy Spirit. Father God and King Jesus will be exalted and lifted high in our midst. No flesh will glory in His presence! He will be our focal point, the tangible substance in our midst. He will have His way in our services and in our hearts.

This movement is for all who will yield to this call of the secret place: spending time with Him. This movement will be for all who are willing to lay aside their agenda and their self-efforts to find Him and to know Him. A cleansing out and a sweeping away of the old theologies and the old mindsets will take place. He will usher in a fresh outpouring of His Spirit with new concepts and new ways of thinking. Miracles, signs and wonders beyond man's anointing will be prevalent meaning HE will show up and move through His presence. As man moves aside, God will do His business by His power. This call and mandate is for His body to seek Him now that He may be found. If our Heavenly Father has the desire to bring a revolution to His body of Christ, He is also looking for willing vessels to usher in His movement and His kingdom here on earth. If we are called to bring God's kingdom from heaven to earth, then He is looking for willing vessels.

Father God has the answers to all of life. Many would agree with this fact, but few seem to understand how to find those answers to the world's problems. Instead of consulting Him, we tend to rely on experts in the various fields of study to help us. Certainly, these experts have a place; however, we must remember who the greatest expert is in all facets of life—our Heavenly Creator. Whether the issue at hand involves family, church, business or politics, He has the solutions to life's complications. Often we rely too heavily on the experts and their worldly wisdom to solve life's problems. Because the problems seem too large and daunting, we choose to let the cycle repeat decade after decade.

God is calling His bride to a higher calling and a deeper walk with Him. Answers to life's complicated issues are our responsibilities to help solve. You see, if life is not all about us, we have been given a commission to preach the gospel and to bring God's kingdom from heaven to earth. For that reason, Jesus prayed the following prayer in Matthew 6:10: "*Your kingdom come. Your will be done on earth as it is in heaven.*"

How can we as humans bring heaven to earth? The process starts by knowing His voice and obeying His leading. Knowing Him is attained through spending time with Him. We have been given the greatest resource available—His Word. Through intimately knowing Him, we can be used to bring change and lasting fruit to the world in which we live. Every Christian must accept this responsibility and be held accountable to this calling, Each one of us has a great responsibility to bring change in our sphere of influence in our homes, churches. workplace and cities. We were never created to be followers; rather, we have been called to lead and to carry God's transforming presence everywhere we go.

Time spent in God's Word coupled with time spent in His presence will give us the clarity and boldness needed to fulfill this calling. Indeed, we have a "hidden" army in every vocation here in this world. Think about the possibilities for a moment—a hidden army in the business world, the political arena, in churches, in schools and institutions of higher learning, and even in hospitals. Beyond, we have the army of people to fulfill the calling and to bring transformation and answers to all aspects of life through Christ—not because we have any wisdom of our own. Our Daddy God is all-knowing and all-wise because He created all of humanity and the world in which we live. But this whole movement of change starts with every believer being willing to say "Yes" to the clear call to know Him and to take the time to find Him.

We must make room for Him in our lives, homes, churches, and businesses by saying "No" to our increasing busyness and life's distractions and "Yes" to His call and presence. Our King must once again be established in all of these places. The problems should no longer be left for the world to solve. We, as heirs to the King, must ask Him and accept the responsibility to help bring change to the complicated problems that have evolved here on earth. Nothing is too large or so impossible that God cannot resolve.

To bring His resolutions to others, a new perspective and a fresh vision from our Heavenly Father is needed. We must ask Him to renew us to His call and purposes. The missing element in the world is Jesus, and we have the awesome and amazing privilege to bring His kingdom to earth by introducing a hurting world to this life-changing Man. The movement starts with our accepting the call to come and to seek Him for the greater purpose of knowing Him and making Him known.

Family Transformation

Many would agree, even those with a church background, that a distressing breakdown of the family unit has occurred in this nation. Numerous polls and their resulting statistics prove that divorce, teen pregnancy, drugs and alcohol have affected church families as well as the general public. Our own free will and choices ultimately become the defining factor in these negative events. No doubt the call from our Heavenly Father to bring about change in our families is desperately needed. Through family worship and soak times coupled with His Word, change can begin to take place. For many families, the lack of time has become the defining factor. The answer to this problem is establishing a time fast and then continuing on the new path of soaking together. Unfortunately, we sometimes feel the need to compete with friends, peers, colleagues or neighbors. We feel fearful of saying "No" to certain activities due to the concern that our children may miss out on opportunities, fall behind or fail to become well-rounded individuals.

The following questions may help in sifting through those thoughts. If you are not a busy family, some of these questions may not apply to your household. Ask God to help you with truthfully answering these questions and ask Him for His opinion on these issues.

- What is driving you to be overly busy?

- What is driving you to allow your children to be overly busy?

- What is your family's purpose here on earth?

- Is your family moving toward that purpose or away from it?

- What can you as a family eliminate from your overly busy schedule to enable you to spend more time with your heavenly Father?

- What duty or task in your schedule is no longer gratifying and undesired?

- Have you lost your joy or fulfillment with certain activities in which you or your children participate?

God is not angry; He is looking for a simple change of heart. Our Heavenly Father extends His hand of love toward us, longing to make His love not only known to us but also to our children. However, to do this, He needs an opportunity and space.

The patterns and habits we form in our family will be the patterns and the habits our children form. If we teach them busyness and show them to live life too full and stressed, they will adopt and pass on the same approach to their families. But if we make room for Jesus and say "No" to the overly busy life, our children, in return, will learn how to manage their schedules and to live life with peace and stability. Most of all, they hopefully will do the same in their homes with their families.

We have a powerful responsibility not only to change our destiny but to help form the destiny for the generation that follows ours. Sketching out family time to soak in Him may seem like a daunting task, and indeed, the process may cause some drama for a season. The need is to look beyond the present day in which we are living and keep our heavenly perspective. Our focus is not the world's attainments or achievements; rather, our focal point is fulfilling our heavenly purpose here on earth—knowing Him and making Him known.

We know activities are not wrong to conduct or enjoy. Only the absence of time spent with God due to a jam-packed schedule makes too many activities wrong. Ask God for His wisdom in this matter, and not only will He abundantly give His mind to you, He will also help implement a strategy for change in your home and family. This family soak time can be weekly or more or less. Let the Holy Spirit lead you in this decision. God is not looking for a ritual; on the contrary, He is looking for a relationship, and He longs for these times of enjoyment. We sometimes unknowingly long for these same things from Him as well.

The time set aside for Him does not have to be long. Start with twenty minutes or more and increase this time as the children begin to understand and engage with the Lord. Allow younger children to draw what God is speaking or showing them. Some may want to write about what God is saying. Others may enjoy dancing in His presence, Grant them the freedom of expression.

This family soak time will build unity, bring peace, and build rich memories with Jesus. Spending time in His presence will help you and your children be grounded and strengthened in your identity in Christ. Knowing Him intimately is possible for all those who are willing to set aside time to seek Him together as a family. As your soak time concludes, you may want to save a few minutes to ask Father God His heart in the area of your family and prayer concerns. This is optional but can be a true blessing. Ultimately, you will sense what would be best for your family on each given soak time.

If you include prayer time, try to avoid lists and worry; instead, let the Holy Spirit guide you and allow Him to lay HIS desires on your hearts. Be open to His voice being spoken through everyone, especially the youngest among you. Ask Him to speak, then wait for Him to speak, and pray what He has spoken to your hearts. As He speaks and shows you what is on His heart, let Him pray through you. Our Heavenly Father desires to heal us, our marriages and our children, but to do so, He needs room to move. Hearing Him speak starts with our simple obedience to seek the One who can bring the healing. Will you make room for the King?

Church Transformation

God's revolution cannot start only in our families; He also desires to move in our small groups and youth groups in the local church. The same concepts that apply to the family apply for youth groups, small groups, and cell groups. (Additional material on this subject will be addressed in the chapter entitled "Stop the Train.") His reviving winds can begin to blow and revive all who are willing to seek Him. Be willing to take the risk to bring change and encounter; then watch and see what God will do! Many of the greatest revivals started with a few hungry people who were willing to seek Him and find Him.

Are you willing to be the one to fan the flame? Are you willing to bring change? Are you ready to break out of the box and lead others to this place of intimacy? Change can start with one hungry heart willing to say "Yes" to Him.

Marketplace Transformation

Many believers have established a variety of businesses, careers and jobs in the marketplace. Whether your position is a CEO, a boss or an employee, you have the awesome privilege to help bring change to the atmosphere in which you work. Along with that opportunity is the availability of the Holy Spirit's wisdom!

Any workplace faces problems that need to be solved and relationships to be healed. Wherever human beings are present, problems seem to be lurking. Your position at your workplace is not your spiritual position here on earth. Your heavenly authority and position through Christ was part of your inheritance when Christ died on the cross, and He became your Savior. He has given you dominion in your workplace—no matter what your earthly position is. Your God-given authority is what He has given you, so you have the ability to effect change and transformation in your workplace.

Some desire a different job, but God has already established you in this environment to help bring change—before He can and will move you on. May the concepts of soaking and seeking God's face for wisdom become the driving force that brings true transformation to your work environment. This designated time could be once a month or more. I believe this transformation can start with you alone or with others who also feel the call. Even in the midst of wanting change, enjoy Him and let this time be about loving Him not seeking answers. Do not underestimate the power of soaking and the atmosphere changes that can result as you behold your Father God and trust Him in faith. Lavishing your love upon Him and enjoying Him changes the atmosphere! From that place of rest, He may begin to show you His heart concerning various circumstances and situations in your workplace.

City and Regional Transformation

With God's revolution still in mind, the concept of soaking and even all-night soaking (watching) with God can transform not only our lives but the spiritual atmosphere as well. What a powerful and encouraging thought! God's Word states in Exodus 14:14, *"The LORD will fight for you, and you shall hold your peace."* Resting and abiding in the presence of our Father God and having faith in Him produces powerful warfare. Worship coupled with soaking in God's presence changes the atmosphere over workplaces, cities and regions. As we behold our King, delighting in His presence and enjoying His love, He, in return, fights for us so we can remain in the place of peace and faith. What a beautiful concept! How easy it will be to push back the powers of darkness and usher in God's presence, light and glory.

God's ways are simple; we human beings merely make the matters of life more complicated. We live in a world that is acting out their frustrations in riots and demonstrations of violence—the fruit of a people without Jesus. The Enemy's counterfeit to God's solutions is acting out their frustrations. If gathering together with one purpose and one focus brings about change, then it is time for God's believers to begin our demonstrations of God's supernatural power and precipitate change and solutions to the world's problems. The time has come for God's people to bring a riot to the Enemy's camp! The world's riots and demonstrations affirm a people's crying out for change and longing for something better. In this world, many individuals are looking for more than their lives have been offered.

Christians have the power to bring change in their cities, regions and states. That move toward transformation starts with a group (large or small) of people gathering to find Him, to know Him, and to let Him begin to change the atmosphere over our nation. These problems are not for the world to solve; God alone has the answers to solve them. We know a big Daddy who can answer any question posed. Now is the time to seek God for answers to problems and to bring people together for the purpose to worship Him, marinate in His goodness and bring about lasting transformation in our regions. This movement will usher His winds of the Holy Spirit into our cities and states.

In 2 Samuel 10:12, God's Word says, *"Be of good courage, and let us be strong for our people and for the cities of our God. And may the* LORD *do what is good in His sight."* Every city has a destiny and purpose; we as believers are called to help the people in this nation's cities to find Him and to walk in their God-given destiny. The time has come to take back what the Enemy has stolen and begin to change the atmosphere over our cities and states. As we behold our King of kings through worship, delight in His love and His goodness and soak in His presence, this mission will be accomplished. The Enemy has sent His counterfeits to disrupt the spiritual realm and to stir up fear. but we serve a more powerful King who brings true transformation and change.

As I have already mentioned, these soaking times can be small groups of people with a heart to see big changes take place in their regions. The frequency of your meeting time could be once a month or bi-monthly; the defining factor would be the leader's choice and the Holy Spirit's leading. Allow approximately an hour for this designated time. As the group grows and becomes comfortable with the soaking sessions, the time frame could be extended.

Following your soak time, allow approximately fifteen to twenty minutes or more at the end for Daddy's heart to be revealed for prayer purposes. This time should not be set aside to pray for people's needs and concerns. If some people are in need of personal prayer, wait until the conclusion of your city prayer session. (Of course, some individuals do need a designated time to be healed emotionally and physically.) Keep the focus on Daddy's heart matters and desires for the city. Then allow the people to share what God is showing or saying concerning their city or state. It may be a vision, a scripture or words from God. Then allow them to pray forth those revelations. You will be blessed with the revelation that God reveals. What refreshing this kind of prayer brings!

If the group grows to larger numbers, remember God moves through our beholding Him. There may be times where you simply marinate, trusting He is moving! Keep in mind that the Holy Spirit comes closer through our words of affirmation to Him! He moves when hearts are loving and longing for Him—not a hunger that is forced and striving, but resting and loving Him.

Are you willing to take the time to see true transformation take place in your city? Or will you sit back with passivity and watch the world struggle? It simply takes one willing vessel who will say "yes" to God's movement.

Questions to Consider

- Have you been passively watching the world struggle with problems (in their homes, churches or businesses)?

- What is God saying to you about bringing change in your sphere of influence? Ask Him and wait for Him to respond. Remember, when He speaks, simple obedience is what He desires.

- Do you believe God has you working at your job or business for a specific reason? What is He saying to you about this matter? How could you bring change to the atmosphere at your workplace?

- Do you long to see God move in your city and state, bringing His fresh move to revive the people? Ask God to dream His dreams through you and show you His desires for the region where you live. Ask Him what you are called to do to help move toward His dream for your city/state.

UNITY—DIVIDING WALLS MUST GO

THE IMPORTANT ISSUE OF unity is seemingly at the forefront of any good leader's agenda. Without being unified, fulfilling the leader's ultimate goals would be nigh onto impossible. A recognized fact among sports teams, businesses, churches, and families is that fighting, competition, jealousy, and pride can hinder the fulfillment of their ultimate purpose.

Through the years, I have watched leaders, including myself, struggle with this issue of trying to accomplish unity. Often behavioral management, self-examination, teaching, control or even threats seem to be the only means used in an effort to bring unity. I certainly understand all of these methods because I have been a leader and a parent. As a general rule, the control tactics and threats do not bring positive change. At times, we can see some results and change, but leading can be wearying and hard.

I have found that the most beautiful fruit of unity comes when each individual takes his eyes off of himself and sets his gaze upon

King Jesus. When a person truly gets in the "zone" with God, much of the bickering, fighting, complaining and irritation begins to disappear. The focus becomes all about Him—not about *me, my rights* or *my desires*. If seeking the presence of God becomes a repeated practice, divine unity begins to become the fruit of this divine connection—God to man with a heart-to-heart connection over and over again.

What man desires to have is God's peace and unity, but it's virtually impossible to acquire this in the natural. Rather, acquiring His peace and unity has to be a supernatural work of the Holy Spirit's changing hearts, minds and spirits to ultimately becoming unified and one with Him. For this reason, His presence and character is so valuable in our lives. We may try as hard as we can to bring about this supernatural work in the natural—to no avail. The task seems far too difficult, frustrating and exasperating. God never intended for man to try to bring about unity through the flesh.

At this point, faith in His Holy Spirit plays an important factor as we seek His presence without an agenda to change the people we are leading, but looking to Him to do a supernatural work that we cannot do in the natural. Gathering together as a group brings about the transformation that we long to see in the people God has given us to guide. God begins to tear down those dividing walls in our hearts sometimes without our even knowing it. Strained relationships become peaceful because He is the Prince of Peace, and His peace begins to permeate in and through us. Those dividing walls that seemed impenetrable begin to crumble. Hearts relentlessly full of themselves begin to soften in the presence of our loving and tender heavenly Father. The love that we experience from Him is carried forth, and we begin to exhibit that same love to those around us. His supernatural work surpasses our intellect and brings healing and restoration in ways that could never be accomplished in the flesh. This divine work is beautiful and very refreshing!

In America, Christians have the wonderful privilege of choosing which church they wish to attend. Many distinctive denominations and doctrines have been established in these different churches. They begin to become the dividing walls that hinder the body of Christ as a whole from becoming one and at peace with one another.

I can see a parallel picture taking place in many of the churches in our cities across the nation. The parallel is similar to many familiar businesses competing to win their customers' favor through the medium of advertising to increase sales and build a returning customer base. I sense that some churches are unknowingly competing with one another within their cities with a similar focus—growing the church and building their own kingdoms. Could it be that in busily building their own established church that they have unknowingly lost the focus that they are a small piece to the large puzzle in the body of Christ? It takes all—every denomination—to make up His body of Christ. It's really not about our local church and our sole agenda that matters. When looking at unity from a heavenly perspective, He sees us as one, and even with all of our unlovely, competitive qualities, we are really beautiful to Him.

This word *competition* was ringing in my ears one day after returning home from church. This powerful word being released to me caused me to examine and begin thinking differently about my own life as well as the unity that God wants to bring throughout our cities. The following is what He spoke to me that day:

Competition is not what you are to pursue. Comparison is not of Me. Constant glances over your shoulder never makes you better.

They are only a reflection of the inward battle to be great. You seem to forget true greatness comes from Me, your God.

Do you understand the power of love? Love not only washes away your sins, but it covers all mistakes and even develops a sense of awareness of My Holy Spirit. When competition, comparison, jealousy and envy are present, you tend to be unaware of My presence and My Spirit. Where is your dwelling place? Do you dwell in the river of life or wallow in the mire of comparison?

Perfect love comes from Me, and when you constantly abide with Me, you become more aware of My desires. You begin to carry My heart to the rest of the world. Your fleshly cares drop away, and My presence renews, refocuses and imparts strength. Faith and grace to forgive and love are then released and treasured.

There is not a measuring stick to compare you to anyone. I sent My Son, Jesus, who stands before Me to execute righteousness and justice. What I have for you is love. When you love Me, in return, you will receive divine protection from Me.

Psalm 91:14-16, "Because he has set his love upon Me, therefore I will deliver him; I will set him on high, because he has known My name. He shall call upon Me, and I will answer him; I will be with him in trouble; I will deliver him and honor him. With long life I will satisfy him, and show him My salvation."

Even among our churches, people struggle with the need to be noticed and therefore compete with one another. Many who do not understand their God-given anointing or identity in Christ struggle and compare.

A repeated bathing in His presence begins to change and establish the insecure heart. The inverted mindset begins to look beyond his world and can become a person who encourages others, instead of focusing on striving and competing. The fight to be on top wanes in the presence of our King because He is on top—not us! When a child of God is secure in that position with Him, the fight subsides and He brings rest to our unsettled soul. We really have nothing to prove when He is close to us, and we know how loved we really are by Him.

With the subject of competition still in mind, the above word from God began to stir many questions within my hungry heart. I longed to see citywide transformation and a revolution of time and true revival begin. I began to dream and ask God to move in our city and states and nation and bring His love to us.

What would Christ's body look like if we could get past our differences to embrace those with different traditions or doctrine than we believe? What would it look like if we began to seek Him for His greater purpose? Advocating the doctrine of those who are not professing Jesus Christ, Father God and Holy Spirit is not what I am professing, though they may find Him in God's presence too. I am speaking of people who are truly seeking God and loving Him or are on that journey to find Jesus. Some who have not yet found Him are still seeking.

Not out of spiritual pride, but with a pure heart and desire, we must see God's purposes accomplished. The place for citywide transformation is with churches beginning to gather to see evangelism and a movement that is ordained by Father God. What fun it would be to see God begin to sweep across the cities and our nation once again! His unified presence is the key to unlock this door to a movement in your city. Catholics, Presbyterians, Evangelicals, Baptists, Methodists, Lutherans, Pentecostals, Episcopalians, nondenominational and beyond are all members of the body of Christ. For those who are willing to take part and soak in His presence, gathering all together as one will bring a beautiful unity within your city. As a result, the atmosphere and spiritual climate in churches and the atmosphere over your city will begin to change.

This transformation may seem like an overwhelming project, but I must ask this question: is it not overwhelming what each church is individually trying to do? How does that practice seem to be working? Are you experiencing divine unity within your church? Do you see divine unity among all the churches in your city? Or are the churches independent with walls erected? Are you one body of Christ working together to fulfill God's purpose in your city and here on earth?

Perhaps you could honestly acknowledge one of these questions and agree that unity is needed in your church/city. As you have read throughout this book, soaking in His rich presence is where restoring that unity can begin. If you experience that unity in your church and you have the desire to see God move in your city, maybe you are the one to help bring this movement to your city. More than likely, it will start with a few people, but God will do mighty works if you give Him room to move. He simply waits for the invitation to move. We can talk about a movement or we can usher in one with Holy Spirit leading the way.

My challenge would be to lay aside any predetermined agendas and tear down any dividing walls that you may have erected. Ask God to give you a fresh vision and renewed passion for His presence and His perfect will. Let Him show you creative ways to bring this unity that you desire in these places of your life. Whether it's in your church, your family or your business, He will be faithful to respond. Ask Him to show you your purpose and what He has asked you to do to bring positive change in your sphere of influence. Ask Him to give you His heavenly perspective so you can bring His kingdom here to earth. And then simply follow His leading!

Questions to Consider

- Do you find yourself comparing yourself and competing with others? Ask God to show you what lie has been assigned with this competition. Ask God to replace the exposed lie with His truth.

- Ask God to give you an encounter or revelation that reveals how He feels about you and how strong He makes you in His presence.

- Is there an issue in your heart that hinders unity in your home, church or business/job? Are you willing to give up your rights to bring peace? How might this new attitude bring unity if you allow your rights to be surrendered?

- Do you see or feel dividing walls in your church? If so, ask God to show you how to help with that current condition.

- Do the churches in your city have walls built up? Is God asking you to do something to facilitate change and unity? Be open to His creative heart.

CHAPTER TWELVE

STOP THE TRAIN

E VERY HUMAN HEART YEARNS and longs for intimacy and friendship. God created us with this void so that we would find Him and be filled and satisfied with Him. Part of our DNA dictates that insignificant, minor pleasures only bring momentary satisfaction, and we are always searching for something new to bring us gratification. Unfortunately, this desire does not change when we are born again. Though rebirth takes place in our spirits and we experience positive changes, we still crave and hunger for relationship and intimacy. Our born-again experience is exciting and fun, but over a period of time, the newness "wears off." Though our world has changed and we make better choices, without intimacy with God, we are not totally satisfied.

Deep inside every soul is a gnawing reality that life must offer more than "this," and so begins the search for the good or the bad. Sometimes believers begin making wrong decisions and find themselves on a collision course with old patterns and sins, choosing situations that they know to be wrong and unclean. This innate desire is not an excuse for wrong behavior. Like we train our children, we, as leaders, must help direct God's people in the right way and help them stay on track. Our human tendency is to lose our focus and to get off track.

Every human unknowingly has a deep longing in his heart to be intimate with his Heavenly King. I believe the rise of sexual perversion is directly due to the Enemy's introducing his counterfeit to fulfill this longing in the heart. The world is crying out for intimacy, but that void is only fulfilled through a relationship with God—the only One who will truly bring fulfillment and contentment to these longing souls. Unfortunately, many will run from one thing to another, not realizing that He is the only One who can and will feed and fill the longing soul. Restlessness and dissatisfaction is deep in the human heart until God becomes our closest Friend. We may have everything in the world's eyes, but without intimacy with Him, we are lonely and left feeling empty.

Salvation is mandatory, but we cannot stop there. We must lead God's people to that place of spiritual intimacy and knowing Him through encounters and experiences with His Holy Spirit. But first, we must know Him intimately as leaders ourselves. Next, our job as the body of Christ and God's leaders is to redirect the seeking back to Him. Counseling and therapy are needed, but intimacy and soaking time with our Heavenly Father coupled with counseling will speed up the healing and wholeness process.

A discontented state exists in today's body of Christ. Make no mistake! Our Heavenly Father is drawing us into the throne room near His heart so we can meet and encounter Him. God is calling churches and leaders to establish sanctuaries for Him so He can come, move and rest in their churches. Churches and individuals will make way for the King to come and sit in their midst—that He might have His way.

His children will experience Him in a deep way, and they will begin to experience rich fruit and His deep presence in their midst.

This call is for individuals and churches of every denomination— not for a select few. He is calling us to stop the train and redirect our focus back on Him so the people we shepherd can find Him. Because every church has a specific call, every church appears to be a little different. But this call is for all who desire to see Him move in a powerful way among His people in their church.

The Enemy may whisper a subtle lie in your ear to try and stop you from moving forward with this new way of thinking. The lie he promotes is that your congregation or the individuals whom you are leading are not ready for change. They may need time to get prepared or mature. That lie is as crazy as saying an invitation for salvation is not good for a specific person because he might not be able to handle it! We would never believe that! Why? Because the Bible says *now* is the time for salvation (2 Corinthians 6:2). True, we cannot control how a person will respond to an invitation, but we certainly shouldn't withhold the invitation. Why would knowing God more personally be any different? He will heal, strengthen, mend and empower individuals. Who would not be ready for that?

Be mindful of the lies coupled with fear that may begin to bombard your thinking as you begin to move in this new way. Oftentimes, leaders want to avoid any difficulties so they take the "safe road," but safe scarcely ever brings positive change. The safest place we can be is where our Father God is leading and directing us. The people will be touched, and tears may stream down their faces or show other signs of God's moving. That outcome is positive! When people are lovingly led with peace, most will understand that when our wonderful Creator touches our finite hearts, tears are a normal aftermath.

Lie 2

Another lie that the Enemy throws at believers is that emotions are wrong in the church—labeling these displays as "emotionalism." Suppose I were to tell you that in your relationship with your family members, no display of emotions or affection could be revealed or shown to them. How do you think your relationships would end up? We can all agree that probably a coldness, an awkwardness, a very unpleasant and mechanical relationship would exist! Let's not let our relationship with Holy Spirit and our churches end up with this wrong mindset and atmosphere! This sterile environment can kill the loving embrace of our heavenly Father.

A time fast may be essential to find clarity and a clear sense of Daddy's call and vision in this unique hour in which we are living. Traditions and religion are not satisfying God's people; therefore, change must take place. If we feed them and lead them to the only One who will satisfy, all of His goodness can be given to His people. The true fruits of the Spirit can begin to manifest through His people once again. More knowledge of Him does not change the human heart; rather having encounters with God and spending time with Him in His presence and loving His Word transforms us.

Teaching the Word will always be important and essential, but this teaching alone is not enough! We must know Him intimately and learn of His heart as we bask in His presence. The local church, which has adequately accomplished the task of teaching about Father God and Jesus, has even laid the foundations of serving the people around us— both inside and outside of the church.

The local church has adequately taught behavior management and God's foundations. All of these areas are noble tasks and deserve recognition. These teachings will always be a part of the church. However, if we never move to the next step, Christ's body will become static and stagnant. If we do not establish the higher calling in our churches, we are missing the greatest ministry to which God has called us: serving Him through His presence and ministering to Him. Serving Him means laying aside our needs or desires and focusing on God's desires. We cannot become satisfied with teaching and serving alone. Establishing a place for our Heavenly Father to be ministered to personally is the missing link to the fresh outpouring that God wants to bring to His people.

The body of Christ has been so busy tending to themselves that they have become apathetic toward the One for whom they profess to be doing all of these tasks—Jesus. If you serve as a leader in your church, ask yourself the following questions:

- Is Jesus the pursuit of your services or is your pursuit centered around people and their needs?

- Is the focus of your services more about agendas, life management or church growth?

You may feel confused by these questions, especially if you have a pastor's heart. Yes, serving the people and caring for them is vital for the church, but the heart issue that becomes important is to what or who we are leading the people. If the Holy Spirit, Jesus and Father God are not the pursuit and the centerpiece of the church, the vision may need to be readjusted. If the main pursuit of the church is growing the numbers of attendees and simply tending to their many needs and the pursuit of Jesus is the minor focus, it may be time to establish a place for your people to refocus their gaze back to Jesus.

Meeting the needs of people will always be important as will be church growth. But hunger for Him must be encouraged through soak times. Often our services tend to turn our focus back on the people and their needs and off God. Life is not all about us! Jesus is the most important Person we can serve. Even the most hurting among us can find healing by giving their affection to their heavenly Father.

Scheduling times for God's people to be refreshed and to let God encounter them without man's intervention is extremely necessary. Deep spiritual needs can be met as we turn our eyes from ourselves and fix our gaze on Him. Along with that, as He becomes the focal point and His presence becomes tangible and rich, church growth will be automatic due to the Holy Spirit's presence and drawing. He is the One to establish first, and He becomes the most important Person to whom we minister.

Matthew 6:33 says, *"But seek first the kingdom of God and His righteousness, and all these things shall be added to you."* What does *"all these things shall be added to you"* mean? The context of Matthew 6 would indicate that *"all these things"* refers to what we eat, drink, and wear. Indeed, God knows that we need food, water and shelter. But I believe that Matthew 6:33 *could also* include healing, deliverance, spiritual growth, church growth and all that we long for God to do for us as well as the people we are leading. *But I believe seeking Him first is the key to these rich blessings.*

In no way are we to throw all outreaches and established ministries unless God instructs us to do so. But taking the concepts of soaking and building an altar to the Lord and giving God's people time to marinate in His goodness is the key to unity and oneness for Christ's body of believers. It is not a quick fix to change the people, but the regenerating work will begin and over time the fruit will begin to be seen. Your corporate soak session should be a consistently scheduled meeting conducted once a month or more often if preferred. These set times should be with an emphasis and a brief explanation on the concepts of soaking.

Why do we practice soaking? Remind God's people that this set time is for them to minister to their Lord through worship. Additionally, it is God's time to minister to them; they simply need to receive and enjoy Him—nothing more. Share how much God loves them and longs for their time to be with Him. Remind them of His deep longing to be with His children! After all, He has been pursuing His children for years! Remember this time is not for long teaching and man's anointing to flow. We simply need to usher in the Holy Spirit and let Him lead and prompt. If He does not ask you to do or say anything as the leader during this time, relax and receive from Him also.

This time is for God to do what He does best—love His people and show Himself mighty to them. We leaders must step aside and allow the Holy Spirit full reign during His time. If God gives you a single scripture, read it and go right back to soaking. Long explanations and excessive talking during these soak times can hinder God's Spirit from freely flowing. Trust Him! After all, who better than He knows how to minister well to His people? Allow God to do His deep work by His Spirit and watch Him move on people's hearts. You see, God makes establishing a relationship with Him easy; we are the ones who seem to make matters complicated.

Leave personal prayer, prophecy, and healing for another designated time. If you see the need for people to receive personal prayer, schedule another service with soaking, healing and prophecy as the focus. You will find the soaking ministry is to flow through every ministry, apostolically speaking, concerning church order, meaning leadership meetings, business meetings and healing services. Everything we do can have a lasting effect when the throne room of God is the anchor of the church.

God will lead and give orders and directives if we give Him space to do so. It truly is beautiful. Adding soak time to all of these ministries will enhance His anointing and bring lasting changes.

At the end of your soaking time, you may want to pray for your city, your church or some matter that God has placed on your heart. As I have already mentioned, try to refrain from personal prayer and need; this time is to seek God's heart for your church or city. Cast the vision to the people for the prayer time. For example, you might want to say, "We will take these last twenty minutes to focus on praying for our church. Seek God to reveal His heart concerning our church and what He desires for us to pray about concerning our church."

Allow some time for seeking and then allow any revelations from the people to flow. Give them time to pray the Father's heart concerning those revelations. This prayer time is optional but very beneficial. You may want to have this soaking time to be only a time for God's people to receive and minister to their Lord. God will show you, the leader, what your people need during this season.

The following was a powerful word that God gave me that correlates to this subject:

> Trust Me that you would know the depths of My heart. When you trust Me, you are taken to deeper realms with Me. Your fear holds you back from knowing My ways and My heart. All that I desire to show you is wrapped inside of this issue of faith and trust in Me.
>
> Often My children fear rejection, so they withdraw from pressing into knowing My true heart over the countless issues of life. They retreat with presumptions about how I would probably perceive the situations they were experiencing in their lives. The result becomes

a disillusionment of who I really am, which hinders My true heart from being revealed.

Children, you must allow Me to conform and transform your thinking. Allow Me to break old mindsets and lies so the truth of who I really am can shine through. The best remedy for an improper mindset is an encounter with Me. The minds of My children are full. But true encounter is the best cure for this overactive, cluttered mind. When My radical love begins to move on the dry and thirsty heart, truth begins to blossom and faith is renewed.

Questions to Consider

- Can you think of people in your church or life who would benefit from soaking in God's presence? Ask God to bring their faces to your mind.

- Would you be willing to bring them to a soak service or start a soaking time on your own?

- Nothing is impossible with God. Ask Him to show you His dream for your church along with the calling for your church. By faith, believe what He told you is true.

- How do you fit in this dream that God has for your church?

HEAVENLY
PERSPECTIVE

W ITH EVERYTHING HAPPENING IN the world today, one of our greatest battles can be to maintain our heavenly perspective, i.e., balancing the darkness concerning the world views with God's heavenly perspective and opinions. Renewing our minds through God's Word and His presence helps us to keep God's viewpoint at the forefront of our lives. I think of it like this: I need glasses to see clearly. Without them, everything appears a little blurry. Availing yourself of God's presence and His Word is like putting on His eyeglasses and seeing through the light of His beautiful heart. His presence and Word washes us and cleanses us from the debris and filth that we pick up along the way simply by living in this world. Spending time with Him is like taking a spiritual bath and being cleansed daily. *cleanse* Without encounters with Him and His Word, the residue begins to build up, leaving us with a hazy mindset and a skewed perspective... and maybe even a little stench!

As I have maintained throughout this book, we are living in a new season. God's Word warns us of this new season in 2 Timothy 3:1-5, which says,

> *"But know this, that in the last days perilous times will come: For men will be lovers of themselves, lovers of money, boasters, proud, blasphemers, disobedient to parents, unthankful, unholy, unloving, unforgiving, slanderers, without self-control, brutal, despisers of good, traitors, headstrong, haughty, lovers of pleasure rather than lovers of God, having a form of godliness but denying its power. And from such people turn away!"*

This Scripture aptly depicts the days in which we are currently living. Since darkness, unfortunately, is the world's view and perspective, why should we expect anything else? Darkness, which is the absence of light, can still espouse twisted half-truths that seem to be close to right. However, usually lurking in the background and at the heart of the matter, that darkness is rooted in error.

I think all of us can admit we have watched each one of these sins named in 2 Timothy 3:1-5 escalating and evident in ever-increasing measures. Part of our warfare is having the ability to see the problem clearly, identify it, and refuse to allow these half-truths to begin to take root in our own heart. Deception seems to be the deep root that causes many of these manifesting spirits. Being aware of how this spirit works and operates is key to staying free from these sins. Obviously, deception and lies are the polar opposites to God's Word and His truth. The remedy is God's presence and His Word coupled together. Understanding the spirit of deception will help us navigate in this dire hour.

God gave me a powerful vision years ago that helped give me a visual and spiritual image of how the Spirit operates. In my vision, I saw a Christian individual standing with a hand mirror in his hand. As the light of God's Word, His truth, or His presence would shine toward the heart of that individual, he would choose to sometimes deflect the light with the mirror. When the person would deflect that light, he would aim the mirror at another person, tagging him with the sin that Holy Spirit was trying to reveal in his very own heart!

This vision was a revelation to me—not only to be clean of the spirit of deception in my own heart—but understanding how that spirit operated in the lives of those around me. Oftentimes, the spirit of deception will accuse others of the very sin that has a grasping hold in their own hearts. Unfortunately, those who are entertaining the sin believe they are completely clean and free from the very sin they have assigned to others. Understanding this simple truth helps us live righteously in this world. We are seeing confusion all around us through false accusations that seem to be manifesting through media, riots and all of the complicated relationships people experience personally and socially. Having the ability to understand and discern the truth from the lies helps us to have heavenly perspective on these issues.

I believe deception begins out of a heart that does not fully understand his identity in Christ and the intense love that the heavenly Father has for him. For others, repeated hurts without healing have made them touchy and wounded. One more life issue may make them feel like they will lose it, so some defend their hearts and deflect any and every truth or correction that will make them feel weak or vulnerable. Defensiveness is a protective mechanism to hide the pain. They may have heard with their ears how much God loves them or even considered the matter, but the deep encounters have not overtaken them.

Leaders, one of your pursuits should be to see the world transformed by HIS love—not by our love for them. Leaders must gently expel the darkness through leading them to the light and showing them that Jesus loves and does accept them fully. Encounters with God do what man cannot, bringing deep healing through life-changing experience. Such experiences cannot be written off. (For some extreme cases of deception, intense counseling coupled with encounters will be needed to bring wholeness and freedom. Ultimately, rejecting deception and the lies of darkness is an act of the individual's will.)

When Jesus is the One truly being lifted high and He becomes the pursuit, deception begins to lose its power. When God is the focal point and the attention is drawn away from man and back to what is important, our skewed vision becomes clear. He is our Focus and pursuit! No matter what the conflict is, Jesus can steal the show with His presence and goodness. Churches, families and beyond can be healed from the sins of this age and the deception that is so prevalent around us.

After many years, I believe it is now time to release this vision that was given to me from God in 2008. I believe what God gave to me has begun to unfold, and we are now seeing the manifestations from this warning. This vision was not lofty, but simple and clear—the way our Father seems to speak to me. Thankfully, He also had a solution to reveal with this vision. I could see the map of the United States. Over different regions of our country, I could see heaping layers of darkness. Some regions were thicker than others.

The Lord spoke and said that these layers of darkness represented the belief systems that people have embraced. Some of the covering darkness was not simply from present-day beliefs but dogmas from the past generations that have been handed down. Nonetheless, they were there. I could see four very distinct unclean spirits that were being released over our nation:

- Oppression which causes discouragement and keeps people from hearing God's truth and from fulfilling God's Great Commission.

- Resentment that would manifest through anger and offensive ways. The Lord said that these spirits would escalate, and MAN would not be able to stop the spiraling effects of the offenses and anger. He even spoke of the people's publicly showing fits of rage. He revealed that the light and darkness would be extreme.

- The third spirit was idolatry.

- Lastly, I saw the spirit of deception being released.

You may wonder, "Why are you sharing this vision now?" This prophecy is now being lived out before us daily!

Thankfully, the best of the vision is yet to come. We have an opportunity to live out prophetic destiny and change the spiritual realm and help fulfill God's perfect will in America. I began to see places being established all throughout the nation where people would come to soak and encounter the love of Jesus and pray. When people gathered to soak in the light of His presence, the deep darkness over their cities, regions and finally the nation was gloriously expelled. The more groups of people who would gather with the purpose to seek, encounter, and behold Him, the greater the light that was released. Soon the light overcame the darkness!

God anticipates doing a supernatural work among His people. The time has come for God's people to change the course and the direction in which our world is heading. We have the power to bring change and transformation in our churches, cities, states and ultimately our nation. The time is now! Our season has come to rise up and take back the ground that the Enemy has tried to steal. Oppression, resentment, idolatry and deception, along with all of the other unclean spirits, do not have to be the driving force in our nation and cities or churches.

We have been given the authority to have dominion here on earth. Through the cross and price Jesus paid for us, we have been given the grace and power to bring spiritual change wherever we go and live. It is what we do and who we are.

Isn't it time to let God flex His spiritual muscles and show the world who is really in control? Letting God be the center and the focus in our midst will usher in His movement here on earth. I believe that we all could agree that matters do not magically change; a quick fix is usually unavailable. Diligence and faithfulness are the keys to transformation. We simply obey the Holy Spirit, and HE will begin to unravel the unseen spiritual realm and make all things new. This does not have to be intense warfare but simply making Father God most important in our meeting times once again.

With heavenly perspective still in our thoughts, my challenge to you would be for you to dare to ask God the simple question I asked my heavenly Father one day prior to His call for me to write this book. I asked, "What have You, Daddy God, called me to help fix and appropriate change here on earth? I know You have a divine purpose for me. How might I help You here on earth?"

Questions to Consider

- Ask God to expose any lies and/or deception that you may be believing. Wait in His presence and give Him room/time to speak. He loves to see us free, which is why He reveals the truth and exposes the lies.

- Have you been deeply wounded by someone or by a circumstance? With God's help, do you think you could forgive the people or persons involved with your pain? (If you feel caught in your pain, you may need to ask for someone's assistance to pray with you and help you work through this process.)

- Once you have forgiven, ask God to release His healing to your heart over that situation. Ask Him to show you His heart considering this situation. (If you are struggling, ask someone to pray with you to help bring this emotional healing.)

- Are you willing to move toward God's desire to push back the powers of darkness through soaking prayer?

- Ask God for His heavenly perspective and what changes and beliefs you have that may be skewed and need adjustments.

CARRIERS OF HIS
GLORY AND PRESENCE

WHEN THE PRESENCE OF God becomes a lifestyle, your heart will be yielded to His perfect will. With that heart-to-heart connect, His heart's desire soon becomes your heart's desire. At this point, oneness in the Spirit begins to take place. His Holy Spirit becomes your greatest reward and your sought-for treasure. Seeking Him and knowing His will is the ultimate quest. Bringing our Father comfort and knowing His desires and His will above ours seems to be the cry of the heart. Once this divine unity begins, the oneness is beautiful and highly esteemed. Life that was once all about me begins to change and becomes all about Jesus.

When this divine connect happens, we become keenly aware of who is living within us and who wants to make Himself known through us. Knowing how loved we are by the King of kings is a coveted position of the heart as well as a place of rest and faith. The reality of who is living within us and understanding that we are never alone changes our perspective and the way we live our life here on earth. After all, if the greatest Revivalist, King Jesus, abides in my soul and lives within me, nothing is impossible. The revival I carry within me can flow from me at any time. Understanding, believing and trusting that we are a chosen vessel for Him is a position of the heart,

From this position, we can rest and abide and stay in that place of peace with our Lord. With one ear listening to Him from His heavenly perspective and one ear listening to what's happening here, we can be used to bring healing, change, blessings, prophetic encouragement, wisdom and knowledge to those around us. That's how we bring God's kingdom from heaven to earth. Jesus' prayer in Luke 11:2 says, *"...When you pray, say: Our Father in heaven, hallowed be Your name. Your kingdom come. Your will be done on earth as it is in heaven."* Releasing His kingdom or anointing and presence wherever you go is part of His perfect will for each of our lives. You are in a position of knowing who lives within you, listening to His still, small voice and being bold enough to obey Him.

Abiding with Him is a state of being keenly aware of His indwelling Holy Spirit and having a heart that is at peace and rest, knowing full well that He is in control and will never leave or forsake us. Abiding in Him can be challenging as life can bring about obstacles and circumstances that scream everything but peace to us. Positioning the heart in the place of rest, peace and trust can sometimes be an ongoing battle within. But as with anything worthwhile in life, when we practice over and over until this positioning becomes easier and begins to become a way of life. When the natural threatens to take over and your flesh begins to overtake your spirit, you suddenly feel the difference. Unsettled and restless, we can run back into the arms of Jesus and find that place of safety and peace. He helps us find that place of rest all over again.

Keeping the communication lines open between you and your heavenly Father will be key to abiding and carrying His tangible presence with you wherever you go. You see, He is peace, love, joy, and all of the other fruit of the Spirit. Allowing His spirit to flow through us freely allows the fruit of His Spirit to flow through us also. Keeping our vessel pure and clean is mandatory so that we do not cause barriers to hinder the flow of His Spirit with the lines of communication.

Sin always leads to shame, guilt and condemnation. When we sin, our natural tendency is to run and hide like Adam and Eve did in the garden of Eden. Guilt, shame and condemnation take over, breaking our fellowship with Him because we feel unworthy and shameful as a result of our acts. He doesn't change though; His love is the same. However, our mindset changes about ourselves. Running back into the arms of Jesus, confessing our wrongs is a simple solution to keeping the communication lines open and freely flowing.

We can cling to the wrong thoughts and mindsets caused by the shame, guilt and condemnation that we embrace. If we allow these attitudes to prevail, the Enemy will try and heap more on those negative thoughts. An immediate sprint back to Jesus and His indwelling presence is all that He is looking for—not because He needs it, but because we need to clear our conscience and to be cleansed all over again. When we forsake these ways, we have free-flowing communion and union with Him once again.

The same holds true with our earthly relationships. Keeping the communication lines open and clear help us to have peace with our heavenly Father and also with our earthly relationships. Sin, when allowed, will cause broken relationships, wounded hearts and communication breakdown. Staying in that place of communion with our heavenly Father also requires us to have clear and clean consciences before the people with whom we dwell on earth. Being in fellowship with God also gives us favor with the people we live with here on earth.

Releasing God's kingdom to someone we have wronged or brought offence to without an apology or restoration would be extremely difficult. Quickly cleaning up the mayhem we have caused will keep our heart in position to carry His presence. As we do that, the Holy Spirit can flow through us and help us to make a difference in our sphere of influence. In the marketplace, with families and friendships, we can make changes by carrying His presence and glory wherever we go. We can also bring revival and His beautiful presence with us.

We are known in heaven. God releases a beautiful anointing and His fragrance upon our lives as we spend time in His presence. We are known by this fragrance as our worship and adoration is lifted up to Him. He also touches us with a beautiful anointing that is as unique and individual as is your personality and looks. Nobody has the same fragrance because everyone has a different worship and communion and union with their Father God. Each person's fragrance is uniquely and individually crafted in the throne room by time spent alone communing and loving on Him. He releases this beautiful fragrance with His tangible presence that is crafted by Him out of your love relationship with one another. This fragrance is released to you to saturate and permeate everything that you do here on earth, and ultimately, to change your life and the lives around you.

What beautiful things He has in store for us and for all who will come and marinate in His anointing, swim in His river of fun and joy, and savor His parties in His inner courts with Him! As you marinate and soak in Him, you will transform the world around you! I leave you with these closing thoughts.

THE DIVINE ROMANCE

TWO HEARTS BEATING TOGETHER as one is the union of the divine romance. When our heart connects with God's and begins to beat with the heartbeat of the Father, the divine romance has begun. One glance from the Lord and then yet another is only the beginning of your love affair with Him. As you captivate His heart now, He, in return, will captivate yours. His gentle touches, the wisps of His Holy Spirit and His words of affirmation mark the beginning of a beautiful and on-going romance that will escalate and become more and more fulfilling.

We were created for this divine romance; in fact, all of the world cries out to experience this spiritual relationship and union with their beloved King. As one heart yearns for another, so it is with this romance; you long for the Lord, and He longs for you even more. And right when you believe the need in your heart for Him has reached its greatest intensity, another level has yet to be attained. This romance continues and rebounds back and forth from one heart to the other

heart, longing to longing. First, the Lord reaches out and calls for you, then you reach out longing and calling for Him. This love affair will never end and will never be fully complete until we spend eternity with Him. Until then, my friend, I will enjoy this incredible divine romance.

EPILOGUE

JOHN 3:3 SAYS, *Jesus answered and said to him, "Most assuredly, I say to you, unless one is born again, he cannot see the kingdom of God."* If you would like to see the kingdom of God and receive Jesus as your Lord and Savior, please pray this prayer.

> *Jesus, thank You for loving me and dying for me on the cross. Thank You for Your cleansing blood that washes away all of my sins. I believe that God resurrected You from the dead and that You are alive today. Come into my heart, Jesus, and be my Savior now and forever. Thank You for giving me eternal life and for filling my heart with Your love, peace and joy. Amen.*

We would like to hear from you. If you prayed the salvation prayer or if you have a testimony to share after reading this book, please send an email to heavenlyperspectivebook@gmail.com.

Need Help?

If you need assistance in establishing this ministry of soaking in your church, cell groups, business or city, please send an email of inquiry to heavenlyperspectivebook@gmail.com.

Does Your Congregation Need Encouragement?

The Prophets' Chamber is a ministry whereby individuals find encouragement, exhortation and the Father's love being released to His people. As God speaks to us, we, in return, share His loving encouragement to His people. Comfort, strength and encouragement are the fruits of this time spent soaking and waiting for His prophetic words. For more information, email heavenlyperspectivebook@gmail.com.

END NOTES

[1]*Merriam-Webster Dictionary,* s.v. "tarry," accessed June 5, 2017, https://www.merriam-webster.com/dictionary/tarry.

[2]Tim Rowe, "God Is Dancing and Singing Over You: The Wonders of His Love," *Goodness of God Ministries,* https://goodnessofgodministries.wordpress.com/2013/06/02/1911/, (accessed April 28, 2017).

47150374R00077

Made in the USA
Middletown, DE
18 August 2017